Heart to Heart

We Are All Capable Of

Unconditional Love

by Gilles Deschênes

Heart to Heart

We Are All Capable Of

Unconditional Love

4060 Morena Blvd., Suite 109G
San Diego, CA 92117

To order additional copies of this book call:
1-888-BOOKS-08

Cover Design by: Michael Anthony Lynch
Cover Design by: Gennadi Fedorov
Translators: Gilles Deschênes
Nathalie Beaudoin
Carole Morin

ISBN: 1-891099-03-5

Gilles Deschênes is available for lectures and seminars and can be booked through:
Blue Pearl Press
4060 Morena Blvd., Suite 109G,
San Diego, CA 92117
Phone # 1-619-274-7614 or 1-619-406-4006

Manufactured in the United States Of America

Dedication

This book is dedicated to all human beings, especially those who cross my path.

Every human being always teach to others how to reflect more love and I am grateful to you for your great lessons.

Thanks to everybody for existing!

PREFACE

This book about love, was written for all of us. You see, we all live in this world together, and are all here with the same deep motivations: learning to love and creating joy. To invent joy, we all need to love and develop our capacity to feel unconditional love. We are all capable of loving with our whole heart and soul and often we do so without even realizing.

Why is it so important to learn loving? Well... the answer is simple! By opening our hearts to love, we are all assured to be happy... to live our lives in joy... not only for a moment, but all the time.

Our need to love is so important that our heart dies when it is not used to love. We cannot die of love because love is a source of life, but we can die from not being able to love. A heart that is dying to love is sad to see. It shrivels up on itself and withers, and instead of shining, it becomes dull and tarnished. We do not suffer because of loving, but because we so desperately need to learn how to love better.

The face of a human being is like an open book, where all that he has experienced is plainly written. As we read a person's story with the eyes of the soul we actually feel what he lives. Once a person's heart is closed, we also see that his soul becomes sad and this person divided... as if he was in the darkness! As we learn to love, we become more sensitive to the misery of the others, with more compassion and tenderness.

Tears come to my eyes when I think of it. With this book, I wish to lighten the paths of all those who feel lost and are searching for the way to truly feel better.

The heart is designed to love and be happy, not to wither up or hate. Withdrawal and hatred only bring misfortune since they are not natural to the heart and are contrary to what the heart really seeks.

All those whose hearts are dying to love are welcome to cross my path, because it is with joy that they would pour out their sadness and discover that they too, are fully capable of learning to love, starting with themselves. It always comes down to this: "Being with others to become aware of who we are... to continuously perfect our learning to love."

We have nothing to face but ourselves... facing the great challenge of learning to better love all that is around us. All that is found in front of us is only an appearance and an illusion to bring us to this important learning which is hidden behind... because our way of seeing and loving what is around us is only a way to see ourselves and to demonstrate the love we feel.

All my inspiration and creativity flow from love. The outside world is not the triggering element for the love I feel, rather it is the recipient, a simple pretext to manifest love from deep within. Without the love that I invent each day, I could not live.

To be able to write, I need only to feel this love. It is then that the process is automatically engaged and the words flow through one after the other. This is how this book about love was written. Without a single mental effort... no reflection... not even thinking... Why work so hard?...This book was written with my whole heart and soul indeed, with all my being... with joy and enormous pleasure... A real pleasure ride! I felt like being kind toward myself and thus it was accomplished without any effort!... I now feel like sharing with you all the finest treasures I have in my heart...to offer you a deep tenderness as appreciation for what you are.

Writing a book about love is a logical consequence of all we are. It is not possible to write about love when we do not feel it or we are unable to love. In such cases, we can only project the mental side of love, love is transformed by our mind, or should I say, distorted by our minds.

It is much the same as you are reading this book. It can be taken as a new beginning cycle about learning to love, a consequence of your inclination to love which is pushing you to transform yourself. Behind the sentences and the thoughts of this book, are emotions and energies of love you can capture. This energy is available and accessible to you. It does not belong to me, but to all of us and in fact, to the whole universe. This love energy is only here to be shared. By reading on, you can let your emotions awaken you. Follow the feelings of your heart as you read to fully appreciate it! There is no need to think or activate your mind, just let the emotions flow through your heart and relax!

Once we enjoy loving with all its facets, we enjoy seeing love all over, even when it is hiding behind evasions. Seeing love all around us makes our life enjoyable and much more simple. We become visionaries and like magic, all that exists then acquires the possibility of being beautiful and lovable, and, in return, makes us happy.

I am a promoter of love, one of its propagators. I like to live and feel love the way it is in my soul, and tell you how I feel by loving this way. I want to meet the challenge of bringing out my love to its fullest expression from deep within, and I sincerely think you can do the same... if you want to, because I have no monopoly on abilities. You have all the abilities you need to follow my example.

I have written this book for that reason, in other words to share with you the amazing results of achieving just such a goal, as well as how I attained it.

Consequently, I have discovered that I no longer need anything in the outside world to make me happy. I am self sufficient with what I already have inside me. My willingness, my strong inclination and desire to love have taken on gigantic proportions, everything outside me has now become a pretext to love! Even what was not lovable within me has become lovable.

All can be loved; We need only extend our vision for this to happen. All that exists, invisible or not, is worthy of love, because it becomes lovable within itself. By continuing to love, we reach a stage where we can no longer restrain ourselves from loving. Loving becomes stronger than us and stronger than all! Happiness can no longer escape us once we learn to love with such intensity, because all is a pretext of happiness. We even transform our ordeals into exciting new challenges to remain happy!

It is with pleasure that I share with you my story and all that I know about love. I wish you all good fortune... all the happiness there is in loving. Joy is waiting for you like ripened fruit in a tree, it is ready to be picked.

You have all the capabilities you will ever need to love, and my hope is that through this book you will become fully aware of them. You are truly able to enjoy lasting happiness and to live your life in continuous joy.

Find out who you really are and be amazed to discover that behind the superficial layers and appearances, you are a “being of love and light.” It is what we all are from deep within, and it becomes more and more visible with time.

Enjoy the reading!

Gilles Deschênes

Table Of Contents

CHAPTER I

What Do We Really Need?

What type of life plan do we need to be happy?

Do we need love?... Money?... Success?... A gorgeous, sexy, loving, caring partner and to top it all, one who is also a great lover?... Is this the whole scenario that would guarantee us happiness?... To answer these questions, we must identify our most important needs.

What is our most essential need?

What does each human being really need? What is the most important need. Being wealthy?... To live in wealth and opulence on top of having all the pleasure of ones sexual fulfillment? Being loved by a spouse, children or others?... What of possessing glory, intelligence and power?... Shouldn't these be a guarantee of long lasting happiness?...Of deep fulfillment?... Of reaching the top?... A beautiful house, a gorgeous spouse, beautiful kids, wealth, a successful career?... But where is the happiness and sense of fulfillment if they are not included in these attributes? It is very tempting to believe that all of these would provide and assure us of happiness! Nothing seems to be missing! Then, why is it that many people who have all these wonderful benefits in life are still unhappy?

Why do some wealthy people suffer?

In spite of who they are and all the wealth they have accumulated, some rich are still not satisfied. Why do they always want more or admit a desire to change their overall lifestyle?... Why do they frequently want to "leave it all behind" and start a new life, for example?... They would, willingly, "leave it all behind" if they could just attain the happiness and peace which they have not yet found.

> *"I had all one could wish for materially, but I was still living in hell... no happiness and no peace! Only anguish and heartache. I had all I needed to be happy but one thing: I didn't know how to love and I felt very insecure."*

Most wealthy people are in this situation; they seem to have it all but still can't be happy and satisfied! Some are worried about losing all they have accomplished, while others just can't seem to find happiness, and fail to understand why.

Can we be happy without love?

If you were to receive all at once what you wish for, your life would most definitely change. You would be excited and enjoy it for a while. You would have pleasure and this could contribute to nourishing your happiness, at least for a season, but afterwards, your excitement and euphoria would start to wane slowly, if they were built only on that basis.

You would be at the mercy of new sensations, the feeling deep down inside that your heart has not reached the satisfaction you desire, even with all the wealth in the world. Your heart would somehow demonstrate its need for fulfillment, and along with the sensation that it still lacks the same.

A heart's chief necessity is to love. It is only with the love that it produces itself that the heart can grow, expand and be completely satiated; not from other people's love, external excitements, pleasures or pleasant sensations derived from the physical or material world. All the pleasures of life are not sufficient to fill one's heart with joy. It remains half empty and causes us to realize that even with all the wealth we could ever dream of, we still never be happy and satisfied.

Love cannot be bought, we offer it to ourselves.

It's true... you can buy sexual pleasure. But you can never buy love from whoever is giving it to you. Love is free! Even when love is given to you by others, it cannot guarantee you happiness. The love of others can only stimulate your heart to love. If you have already learned to love and are able to do so, there is a good chance you will react by feeling it. But if you have not yet learned to love, it is possible that this love will have little effect on you and your heart will not produce more love; a situation often seen. Even when people are very much loved by others, they can still be very unhappy. Only you can allow yourself to feel love and others cannot do this for you. No one else can love for you, with your own heart, or make you happy against your own will.

If you believe that more money or material goods would certainly bring you happiness or assure you the fulfillment you desire, you greatly need to examine and verify your beliefs in our concrete and physical world. You will soon realize on your own that it is not always fun to materialize so many illusions.

Where to situate our basic needs in our search for happiness?

The basic physical needs must of course be fulfilled in order to enable us to be happy. For that purpose, the basic minimum must at least be assured. Let's not deny this. We all need a roof over our heads, to eat sufficiently and feed our physical bodies.

What we are saying is, if we learn to love with great skill, and if we intensify our inclination to love from the deepest parts of ourselves, we can be much happier. Whether or not we attain our minimum vital needs on a daily basis, we will feel better. That is assured and that is what counts!

Let me say to all who are poor, whether you hail from Russia, from Romania or from somewhere in Africa, that you will be fulfilled with physical benefits once you will be capable to love intensely. God would never abandon its child as he helps himself and proves himself. It is up to you to prove yourself because God is waiting for you to do so, so in turn your needs can be fully supplied.

What is useful about being poor?

It is useful because it helps us learn to appreciate what we already have, and also become more aware that abundance is created by our vibrations of love and gratitude. Once you have learned to love, it is only a question of time before your material situation gets better.

> *"Your physical misery touches me enormously and I often pray for God to relieve you, because I, Gilles, love all of you and I am very sensitive to what happens to you. I have been on this path of misery before, and I know the consequences of being poor. Sleeping in the*

ditch and waking up every two hours during the night to walk and make sure I didn't freeze, was no cup of tea I assure you! This is what I have experienced and I nearly came to perish and die."

But if we love all that exists and accept more of what happens to us, we suffer much less. We create happiness with little things and from nothing, when we do not own any material goods. We can still create happiness because we discover that our biggest blessing and our most important wealth is ourselves and nothing that exists can be worth more. That may explain why we are poor... to primarily begin to discover the treasures hiding within ourselves.

When you become aware of this, you create sure conditions in the invisible universe about the material improvements that will happen in your life. Hating and rebelling against yourself because of your precarious situation and poverty, will do just the contrary. These attitudes will only cause you to attract more misery in your life.

The accumulation of material wealth has good reason to be, once it is used to profit our spiritual wealth.

All that you think you possess on the material plane, you really don't possess at all; and this is the illusion that creates the problem. In fact, all that we possess is lent to us by the Universe and sooner or later, it will change hands. All you own will still remain there after your death, as it is only on loan to help you grow. This is the only reason for its existence and why it is placed at your disposal. The Universe has put it there, so you can increase your "true belongings," you know, the ones that last forever.

What you truly possess is your conscience, your ability to love and your way of loving. They constitute your true belongings and they can grow if you want them to, because there is always room for spiritual growth and you can always increase your spiritual wealth.

It is worth the effort to use the energy that is put at your disposal on the physical plane, to invest it in a precise goal, to benefit your true and real belongings which are those on the spiritual plane. If you restrict yourself to materialistic benefits and increase your material belongings only, you will not truly become richer and you will have wasted a good part of what has already been lent to you. You will in effect, mortgage it! All that you would have accumulated physically will one day slip from your grasp. You will then suffer due to the attachments and illusions you've materialized.

True wealth is spiritual wealth!

Then, why is it that we attach so much significance to our material belongings by acting as if accumulation was a viable goal and a true hunger inside of us?

Why would you believe that what you own is yours and yours only when it is put at your disposal only on temporary basis? It is important to detach oneself from what is appealing on a "temporary basis" only and bears a high potential for attachment, because it is not permanent and hence he represents a high risk for suffering.

We often do this to avoid unnecessary suffering that we will be obliged to face sooner or later in life. We then cease to keep all our thoughts on the materialistic plane and we become available for discovering and appreciating the treasures in our hearts.

You have nothing to lose by discovering and profiting your spiritual wealth. On the contrary, you have everything to win and you will win in every sense of the word! Letting your conscience expand and learning to feel love all the time is a wonderful enrichment that will lead you to continuous happiness. And it will surely contribute to increasing your material wealth.

Material wealth is not a guarantee for happiness.

No wealth can guarantee that the human being will be able to love, abandon or unbosom himself. Wealth can even bore people after a while. But it won't eliminate the need to love which is the function and reason for existing. The first goal is to use all that one has acquired and all that is put at one's disposal to learn to love as well as how to create love.

For a human to be satisfied, the heart must produce love... love that the soul sends... The more a person's heart will produce, the happier and more satisfied he will be.

Only the love that you feel yourself can really satisfy and fulfill you. And this love does not depend on others, nor on things or goods that you acquire. Your heart does not need love that is demonstrated by others to produce and vibrate love itself. It can help but it does not need it.

Your heart has to produce the love vibrations in order for the joy to reach your conscience. What will entice your heart to vibrate love? You will find the answer within yourselves!...That is where it is!...The deep motivation for loving comes from the soul and that is its divine intention. This intention does not depend on material wealth.

The essential is to feel love.

It is not essential to be loved by others, your spouse or your children. The love of others does not guarantee you will feel love or that you will be happy! We often see people who are very much loved by others but who themselves don't know how to love, or what to do to be happy! I've been in their shoes once before. I can tell you from experience that there are many people who feel left out even when they are completely surrounded!

The essential thing is to feel love with your heart. The human being needs to love; he simply cannot do without it! It is absolutely vital to him. Without it, he will suffer and be unhappy. He will deviate from his deepest motivation, which is to love. He will deviate from the intentions of his soul, which will create a conflict in the most subtle and vital dimensions of himself.

This divine intention is at the same time compatible with the motivation on the human plane of each individual. This motivation is that each individual will live his/her life in happiness.

There is reason to be filled with wonder over the greatness of love.

The unconditional love that comes from the soul reconciles the human motivations with the spiritual motivations. They both live together and follow the same direction. The soul wants to rise, and this happens when the human being learns to love and uses his heart advisedly, which will allow him to live his life in joy. Rising happens in joy and with the love that pushes us like a motor in our climb. There is no separation but a beautiful reconciliation with all and who we are. Isn't it magnificent to have access to such great happiness? We only need to change ourselves to make it, and be happy!... Using our heart to love rather than using it to suffer... Using all its power!

What the soul wants and what each human being is looking for, go perfectly hand in hand. What other people are offering you is not guaranteed to make you happy, because all the wealth and pleasures of this earth will never be a source to guaranteed happiness. Sooner or later for different reasons, every potential source could dry up! However, the source of love in your soul will never dry up, neither the liking and inclination to love it will bring to you, and the source of happiness that will result.

Now that is what is essential! That is what will last forever, through time, space, worlds, and all that ever existed or all that exists in the visible or invisible plane for the next hundred years or even millions of years to come.

Why is unconditional love a guaranteed source of happiness?

Because love is global, absolute and holds the energy of all that exists in the physical world. It holds the energy within itself. All that is on the outside is included in the love energy in other forms. Love is an all, complete, where nothing is missing in sensations that are not on the outside of us, or that are not made on the outside.

Love is made in such a way that we can become aware of it as it is in our soul. Not to become aware of it once it is transformed by our mind when it reaches this level or when it is going through our energy flow.

Love embraces any separation because it extends itself to all that exists... things, animals, ourselves, others, even our enemies if we have any, etc... In other words, all that exists, visible or invisible, is put on the same platter to be loved the way it is, all because it has its reasons to be the way it is and there is nothing else to think about. All this is there in our conscience to be loved. There are no value judgments, no hierarchy of what is more or less loved... more lovable or less lovable...

These considerations come from our minds which indicate its preferences. They do not come from our soul. They have nothing to do with the love that we feel. We are no longer confused, because we have learned to see the differences and we know ourselves better.

Our soul holds love for everything, without differentiation and without distinction. We love all that reaches our conscience because we clearly feel the love and because there is enough light in our conscience for us to realize it. It's as simple as that.

We all need to love.

Every individual needs to love. What is important is to help him become aware of this vital need so he can feel it in his body. This is the way he will be able to change his behavior and attitude to feel and reflect more love. Feeling the need to love is not the same as loving. We realize more than before our need to love when our liking and inclination to love grow and that's where we have to start. By stimulating our liking to love! It is often others who do it for us because we are not aware enough to do it ourselves.

Once our liking or inclination to love has grown, it becomes a chain reaction. Our desire for learning to love is solicited at our mind level. We wish to experience love to further perfect our ability to love and be happier. We then develop our ability to love and feel it more. To conclude the chain, it is then natural that we reflect the love we feel in our behaviors. Because of the inflow given by our liking or inclination to love that has grown, the process is automatically engaged and the stages follow through one by one.

The need to love is stronger than any other psychological need.

Even if certain basic needs are not fully satisfied, loving will permit us to eliminate some of the harmful effects that are linked to psychological or physical dissatisfactions.

The need to love plays a major role in life, and no other need can replace it or play an equivalent role. No other need can play a role as fundamental as the one of transforming all types of dissatisfactions into peace and joy.

Love makes miracles! With love, you can make miracles and transform, like a spell, all that surrounds you! It is all a question of time and intensity before you are gratified in all planes simultaneously.

It is a vital need to vibrate love from the heart. We all must do so to be happy, and it is fundamental. By loving, we feel a sensation of joy throughout our bodies. That is very different from "needing love" where the sense is difficult to understand and define.

Sometimes, we think we are loving with our heart, but it is with our mind that we are loving and we misrepresent it. We inaccurately reproduce it from our soul. It results in suffering because true, unconditional and unchanged love that comes from the soul will never make you suffer.

What is the meaning of "needing" love?

Now there is an expression we often hear! This question is ambiguous and has a lot of possible interpretations. What do we mean exactly? What need are we referring to?

Do we need to receive love from others to stimulate our ability to love?... Or then again, to stimulate the activity in our heart when all seems too calm?... We sometimes have the impression that it is too calm and we want more action. Do we need to learn to welcome love?... Or, do we simply need to feel love?...

Like we often hear, the need for love is often referred to by the presence of others who testify their love to us. Possibly, because our love is too poor to enable us to feel it by ourselves without having anybody to stimulate it. Perhaps, we don't know how to stimulate it, even if it has already grown and is rich enough. Therefore, we need the demonstration of others to help us in this aspect. What type of love do we need, when we refer or depend on others to fulfill what we consider a need?

Do we want unconditional or conditional love?

First of all, let us realize that the love we are talking about here is situated on the mental level that divides love in its components and transforms it from its real nature. Most often, we refer to conditional and human love by contrasting it to unconditional and divine love. We have let our mind take over with its logic and have drawn away from our soul:

> *"Love of others is what we need to stimulate us or to make us happy. We need their love. Being happy on our own is too difficult."*

This is what we believe at our mind's level and it is this belief that limits our alternate paths to attain happiness. In fact, what happens is that we hope and want others to demonstrate their love to us because we wish to receive a stimulation that will incite us to feel love. All this just to make ourselves happy! This is often what we mean when we say we need love.

In this perspective, we do not believe that it is very useful to be loved by others if they do not testify it in a concrete way, because we also like to answer back after we have received their love. If others do not let us demonstrate the love we feel for them, we often believe that we feel this love in vain. We see here the mental logic but not the logic of the soul because the love that we feel is never lost and our thoughts of love are always used to bring happiness to others, who capture them. Whether or not others are aware of it makes no difference, because what is important is that this love reaches them and is accepted by some of their dimensions. Even when it can only reach their unconscious, the impact is still real.

The mental scenario of the need for love is frequent and is the particular foundation of conditional love which works like a human business transaction. "*I give you love; give me love in return.*" Conditional love can be considered as a stage we go through to access an immense happiness in the future. It corresponds to a way of loving that can expand and intensify itself.

How do our ways of loving evolve?

Experiencing conditional love is a stage in the apprenticeship of love and loving. We can go further if we want to be happier, independent, self-sufficient, and less vulnerable to the circumstantial jolts of the outside world. Each human being is complete in himself and his need to love is easily adaptable to his conscience that continuously evolves. He absolutely does not need others to feel and live love.

The energy of love, the way it is in our soul, feeds each human with the appreciation and love for himself and love for all that exists. With time, we become able of continuously loving others with our thoughts and without waiting for anything in return.

Love will then extend itself to all that is within reach, and that is part of the inseparable ensemble of all that exists. We are as "communicating vessels" and it is by us that love will extend itself to all the existing components. In other words, the love that everything contains is reunited and it is us who trigger the cycle. We start the ball game. Love is a living and vibrant energy that rises much higher than any human consideration.

And this love is complete within itself because nothing is missing. We often look for something else by saying we are looking for love, but we are in fact looking at ways to learn how to love and we fool ourselves with illusions before understanding and realizing it. We do however realize it with time.

Any one who takes his need to love and brings it to a need for love, from others, and implicates others to satisfy himself is only learning to love and experimenting love on a human plane.

The human being needs to learn to love, to be able to love with all his dimensions.

It's the price to pay to live in harmony. Without love, there is no harmony and without harmony, happiness cannot last.

Every human being needs to love. It is vital to his balance and the creation of harmony. This harmony is created once the individual is able to love with all the components[1] of himself and with a bigger awareness of who he is. He then blossoms and becomes calmer and more peaceful. He is also in a better position to be realized on the human plane, not only on the spiritual plane.

Once the need to love is no longer based on a need for love, implicating others, but instead based on ourselves and simply feeling love, beliefs are enlightened and important lessons are also learned. The apprenticeship of loving continuously evolves and it's only a matter of time before the individual realizes that he has all he needs within himself to feel love and that nothing is missing!

He will then discover the appreciation for himself and his self esteem, in fact, the love for himself. After a while, he will realize that this love makes him more self sufficient and that he can fulfill his need for love without needing others, and without needing to go through them to make it. To love, he will become aware that he can depend on other dimensions of himself, those which are not on the human plane. He had left them aside because he was not aware of their use. All his attention was centered on other people in order to be capable of feeling love. Once having reached this stage, the individual has learned to better know

[1] footnote: The human being is composed of a soul, chakras, a physical body and other invisible bodies. See glossary for the definitions of chakra and invisible bodies.

himself, and his way of loving has gained maturity. He recognizes that love for himself exists and constitutes a development in his way of loving and in the learning process. Then, a point of reunion will follow between unconditional and conditional love, because love for self had prepared him for it.

Love evolves with experience: from conditional to unconditional.

At the very beginning, we use others and the love of others to stimulate our love towards them; it is a stage of conditional love. We then progress to other stages. We realize that it is good to love and we like loving. We realize that we can love ourselves, by using others who stimulate us to love. This stage leads us to autonomy and unconditional love. We then develop the ability to feel unconditional love for ourselves and only need ourselves to feel it! Thereafter, we will be able to extend it naturally to others, even if they do not demonstrate their love for us in return. By loving ourselves with conditions, we then learn to love ourselves without conditions and do it more often. We love deeper and the reason is very simple: Our inclination and liking to love intensifies more and more because we have managed to keep our heart open.

After this stage, we will easily be able to extend our unconditional love to others and to all that exists. To get there, we have nothing to do. Simply be ourselves, because loving others is easy once our inclination to love has intensified sufficiently.

We project ourselves on others all the time. We project how we are. By developing our liking and inclination to love, we can become all and full of love. And when we are able to radiate love with so much intensity, we project it onto others who benefit from it. We don't necessarily do it consciously; we often do it unconsciously with our thoughts or with other dimensions of ourselves that are more subtle.

Depending on the required evolutionary needs of each individual, and what they have chosen to experience before coming on earth, some of us will remain there to further integrate what they have learned. Reaching that point is already a grandiose and colossal progress.

If personal development opens up on the spiritual plane, the evolution of this individual will take on dazzling dimensions. That is because being conscious of our soul is realizing that it coordinates our progress in the apprenticeship of love and that it is, at all times, the instigator of love which we feel even when we are not aware of it.

Realizing the presence of our soul helps us understand how we love.

Realize It! How can you love without even being aware of it? How can you feel love in your heart without understanding why you feel it? Where is the logic in all this? It is certainly not the logic of your mind or brain which is a part of your physical body that will die and terminate with it. What animates you and pushes you to love this way?... If it is not your soul that governs all your dimensions, including the ones you are not aware of yet, what does? How could you stay alive, if it were not for your soul that is in your body?

The presence of the soul or a breath of life in the human being has been demonstrated so many times and in so many ways; scientifically and logically as well as irrationally and illogically. How many people have encountered a "near death" experience and have seen their physical body from the outside as in an astral projection, and yet have returned to recount their experience? How can we see our inanimate body and become aware of it, if all life is finished with the end of the physical body? What makes us become aware of our body on the outside? Are we dead or are we still alive?

The soul feeds the heart that wants to love.

Being inspired to love by our soul allows us to go further with our aptitudes and capabilities to love. We add a larger and more vast dimension to it, which stabilizes the variability in the love we feel. This variability becomes much smaller with time.

We can love with more intensity and in more situations. Our conscience has widened and influences us to intensify our liking and inclination for love. We love stronger and deeper, and we understand the process that pushes us to love, the way we love as well as how to love.

We realize that the unconditional love we feel for ourselves is not limited to ourselves. Since we project it onto others, we finally realize that we love all that exists and do it naturally without needing any support from others. In fact, what we do is simply love and feel love. We even surprise ourselves loving this way without understanding what is happening to us in the beginning.

Once we love with a lot of intensity, there comes a time when our mind is surpassed by the events.

Everything goes too fast for our mind which is surpassed by the events. From a mental point of view, it is hard to explain or to understand what is happening to us. We realize then, that our mind was doing useless separations. It made us believe that there was something else than what we have experienced, that some people could be loved and others not, that there were various kinds of love... In reality, we can clearly see that this is not what is happening and that our mind is surpassed by what is happening.

Our mind can no longer provide satisfying answers. Reality shows us the contrary and it surprises us. We surprise ourselves once we are able to love all that exists. We are astonished by our way of being.

When our liking and inclination for love are intensified, we can no longer differentiate between what can or cannot be loved, as everything becomes lovable. That is why the beliefs and the logic of our mind no longer make sense. Consequently, we adjust our mind to our new conscience by deprogramming it and by putting aside certain beliefs that are now useless. The reality, our attitudes and behaviors demonstrate that love is a whole, unique and indivisible, extending itself to all that exists, visible or invisible. Love, without any separation, is independent of others, of all that exists and of all that can happen.

These ways of being and of doing things are what we demonstrate in our daily activities. We notice it ourselves because we see how we are, and others confirm it to us. Our inclination and liking of love do not come from our minds; it is because of our souls that we can love so much and with such ardency.

To identify the role played by our minds in the process of loving, we have to realize that we have a conscience that can include it, and we also have a soul that can direct our life. How else can we become aware that these parts of us can help us live our lives better? How can we distinguish each role they play? We have to expand our conscience to recognize and accept these important dimensions of ourselves. Without them, we can never understand or explain what is happening to us. It would be harder to find the starting point of learning to love better.

Only the soul allows love to become miraculous.

Our soul is our major strength and it is really powerful. The more we love it, the more we appreciate it, the more we are inspired by it to live our life and the more it helps us to love and clear all obstacles that could block the love we might reflect on the outside. In conjunction with the beyond, it is our soul that triggers the energy flow that allows us to love. Once we show we are ready to love more, the energy we require is sent to us and there are never any mistakes.

In the end, like a miracle, our soul allows us to transform any misfortune into good fortune and any drama into a comedy or otherwise good time.

> *"I personally know some people who have gone through all the stages I have described above. Their stories can serve as examples to demonstrate that you too can evolve and expand your ways of loving. You will then gain a bigger freedom of action while beaming with joy!*
>
> *Even if the path that is leading you there is often full of pitfalls, never forget that further down and behind all of this, the sun will yet and always be shining for you. The path will look like it's in a garden of roses. It is heaven on earth for me! I see it and feel it in my heart. Our soul creates this scenery in pledge for the love for ourselves."*

CHAPTER I EXERCISES

1. INTRODUCTION AT THE LEVEL OF YOUR HEART

- Imagine that your entire being is transformed into your heart.

- Visualize yourself as this gigantic heart and begin an inner dialogue between yourself and this heart.

- Now, contemplate your inner-self and take an objective look at where you are in your capability to love.

HOW IS YOUR HEART?

"Sad? Upset? Hurt? Withdrawn? Filled with hatred, resentment or bitterness? Distressed? Frustrated? Angered? Moody and highly unstable? Does it shut down at the least hardship and obstacle?

On the opposite, is your heart cheerful, so cheerful that it overflows with joy and is unable to withhold its outpourings? Is it on the road to recovery? Is on the verge of opening up? Is it partly open or wide open?

Is it capable of loving? Does it produce love? If yes, how often does it manifest it? At all times? Often or rarely? A little or a great deal?

What kind of love does it reflect? Conditional or unconditional?... Is it a kind of love that has been altered by your intellect or your mind, which interferes in the process that consists of exteriorizing your love as it is in your soul?

Can you feel the grace that inhabits you and which your soul makes available to you at all times?"

Answering these questions will help you to find out where you stand in your capability to love and to feel and express it while living your life.

PREPARE YOUR EVALUATION!

- Make a balance of all your experiences from which you have learned how to love and what lessons you have understood from them, in order to find out what is there left to learn. What other abilities and lessons are still needed to increase your love?
- Refer to entitled section: "How do our ways of loving evolve?" to find out where you stand in regard to the evolution frame that is presented.
- Simply OBSERVE, WITHOUT JUDGMENT the reason it is so.
- Do not judge as good or bad what is left to do or what has already been accomplished.

WHERE DOES YOUR HEART STAND WITHIN THE CONTEXT OF YOUR LIFE?

"Is your heart a source of happiness in your life? What role does it play? Are you fed with love and joy only through other people's hearts?

Does your heart fulfill its purpose as a producer of love? Is it self-sufficient? Does it need others or specific circumstances to be capable of loving? Do you need other people's love for your heart to remain open... to produce and express love?

Is your heart capable of loving without expecting anything from others in return? Is it able to go back quickly to a state of love after being disturbed by some outside event or person? Can it continuously maintain love without being influenced by these disturbances?"

Once you have gone through a true, sincere and objective assessment, be aware of what you just did and allow yourself to feel with all of your body, what your heart has revealed to you so far.

2. VISUALIZATION TO INCREASE LOVE

We suggest that you do the following creative visualization immediately after the preceding exercise.

- Allow your emotions to move freely within yourself without identifying them; let them flow like the current of a river which nothing can stop.

- Accept and welcome any feelings, emotions or thoughts that could follow and thank God for all that happens and exists. Thank also God for what you are.

- Close your eyes and acknowledge to yourself that you are moving across another major stepping stone in learning how to love.

- Imagine yourself reliving an event that was most pleasurable to you in your life. Feel now the agreeable sensations that it brings.

- Feel the happiness growing inside you and realize that you are now happy.

- Accompany these sensations by visualizing that your heart is shining and glowing with light and love.

- Visualize this love extending itself to the hearts of everyone around you, and see the smile appearing on their faces. Imagine it and see the images in your head.

- Visualize this happiness reaching out to everything that exists and that your heart is a huge communicating vessel pouring love into everything in existence.

- Visualize the love in your heart expanding evermore... more and more. It has now gained more strength and is very powerful.

- Imagine thousands of beautiful threads of light reaching out to the angels, the archangels, the mystics, your spiritual guides, the guides of all those who are dear to you, as well as all the spiritual entities that you revere.

- Now, bring your awareness on the plane of your feelings to contemplate your emotions. Look thoroughly into your heart and observe what is happening.

-Repeat as often as you need and notice how your heart improves at increasing its ability to produce more love and to love all that exists.

3. INTEGRATION OF LOVE INTO YOUR DAILY LIFE

As you live your life, use the results of your introspections and visualizations to feel better in your body. By allowing this new level of awareness to inspire you, and by drawing from it a newly created energy, realize how your heart reacts and stands, and how much its well-being rises.

IN THE MORNING, BEFORE YOU BEGIN YOUR ACTIVITIES...

- Tell yourself a warm "good morning," and visualize yourself as a radiant sun.

- Gather your thoughts and center yourself in love. Visualize the opening up of your heart and its rays extending and touching everything that exists, whether tangible or not.

- Set up those ties with your conscience and your mind, and feel that you love everything around you.

- Realize what you have just created with your thoughts, what they create regardless of outside circumstances, or weather conditions, etc...

- Realize that the sun will always shine for you if you choose it.

DURING THE DAY, AS OFTEN AS NEEDED...

- Using your conscience, verify the state of your heart.

- Imagine that your entire being is transformed into a great big heart. Take a few seconds to achieve this transformation and to change your thoughts and feelings to do so.

- If you find blocks or that your heart is closed, go back to what you know, to the state of great well-being you have previously experienced while doing the visualization to increase your love. Imagine this state of great happiness and you will immediately recreate and feel it.

- Remember how much better you felt when your heart was wide open.

- Without thinking and letting your mind interfere, choose to feel love, simply to be happy and to feel better. Change whatever distressing feeling your heart may hold.

- Remember that you are able to love yourself enough to make that choice, and acknowledge, without a doubt, that you deserve to be happy. Remind yourself! Be positive and confirm this fact to you.

- Realize the step forward and the improvement you have just made and say out loud: *"I love and am capable of loving, because I enjoy doing everything out of love."*

DURING AN APPROPRIATE MOMENT AT THE END OF THE DAY...

- Take a moment to contact you and get in touch with the most intimate part of yourself.

- Be aware as to what is most appropriate for you, because this contact with yourself could be made while you are active or doing your daily activities or when you are inactive or passive (whether it is at your workplace, at home or anywhere else that you may choose).

- Empty your mind of all worries and problems that upset you. Leave them behind.

- Realize that the weariness and the fatigue stored and accumulated in your physical body have not been created, nor caused by your heart. It is rather the outcome of your ego which does not know yet how to respect the limits of your body.

- Now, just say a nice "goodnight" to this tiredness and welcome it as a friend passing by who will go away soon; your fatigue is like the sun, setting at the end of a long day.

- Prepare to go inside your heart to review your day.

Have you discovered anything new since this morning? Did you achieve any new understanding about your feelings? Have you learned anything new about love from the opportunities that have been presented to you throughout the day? Were there any learning occasions that resulted and from which you still have difficulty understanding their meaning?

If this is the case, love yourself and choose to feel love, because it is at this precise moment that you deserve it the most. Just say "good-bye" to these potential lessons and that you will go back to them at a later time.

Compassion and mercy will help you. They will allow you to better assimilate these lessons at another time. For now, just be aware of this without judging yourself.

- Continue to contemplate your day from the perspective of your heart and understand its meaning within the context of your life.

- Remember its usefulness: NOT HAVING LEARNED IS A LEARNING OPPORTUNITY in itself, which is to completely enlighten all that has been experienced, in order to prepare the assimilation and the integration of all the lessons which have not yet been understood, but which will be soon.

4. WHAT DO YOU NEED?

Exercise to be done with another person who knows you well (one person asks the questions while the other responds).

Facing each other, you begin the following dialogue.

- What is the point of view of your ego or personality concerning your needs? What does it need? What does your ego want?

- What is the point of view of your heart regarding your needs? What does it need? What does your heart want?

- Are there any differences between the ego's needs and the heart's needs?

- Does your heart and your ego aspire to the same things? Do they progress toward the same goal? If not, how will you reconcile them?

- Identify the differences and take the time to elaborate on each one.

When this step is done, place yourself at the level of your soul to become as if your entire being is only your soul. Then, visualize the solutions. What are they? Elaborate.

When all these questions have been answered by the first party, you should interchange the roles with the second party as a new respondent. Start at the beginning.

When both roles have been played by each party, make a consensus and express out loud what you need.

Exchange with your partner. Compare your answers and your solutions. In which part of yourself do you stand? In your ego, in your heart or in your soul?

To do this exercise, refer to chapter I, that highlights our most essential needs. Try to feel deeply the reasons why it is so.

CHAPTER II

What Is Loving?

Loving is a process that consists of transforming ourselves to feel happiness on a continuous basis. We do that by taming and strengthening our liking and inclination to love. This becomes the ally that brightens the path of our life on a permanent basis. Our feelings are mostly independent of whatever could happen in our life, because they are founded on our love which is now becoming so strong.

The transformations grow from a better knowledge of who we are and by using the strength and the power of our soul to feed our conscience with light. This way, we can create more harmony in our way of being, in our attitudes and our behaviors. The rays of love coming from our heart transform themselves to become stronger, larger and more luminous. For this to happen, we must strengthen the connection between our heart and soul and we can achieve it with our conscience.

Loving is like a goal to reach!

Being this way is not always easy in the beginning because our soul needs to free itself from what is stopping it from being all love in order to help our heart to love. Once our soul has taken its flight, loving then becomes very natural without any effort. The ideal thing would be for our heart to remain open at all times, and let the chakra of our heart play its role fully, and to feed it with energy, without interruption, blocks or bias. This can not be done without the support of the soul.

Loving implicates a large awareness of ourselves and a certain ability to relate to our soul, to feel the vibrations and sensations of joy. We adjust our behaviors to our conscience, which is also related to our soul. Because our conscience is growing, we learn to better manage the use of our heart with the only goal of loving and making ourselves happier at all times.

The connections between the different components of ourselves must be made. It must then be maintained in order to create a certain harmony each and every day, no matter what we have to live through or face. Our liking and inclination for loving contributes to create this harmony and, from that point, nothing can be put aside in our different dimensions (physical, mental, emotional, energetic and spiritual).

It is our soul that brings liking, inclination and desire for loving to the conscience. Having the liking or inclination for loving on a continuous basis is a fruit to an important spiritual route. Once they have reached our conscience, they are materialized by the vibrations and the great sensations of well-being that are felt in our heart and in our physical bodies. This desire and liking for loving have nothing to do with our beliefs nor with our mind. The latter appears only at the end of the process to experience with our inclination or liking to love in the concrete world, so that we can live it in our every day life. Using our mind this way can help us gather more and more serenity and our life can be lived in joy. Peace will come because the roles of the different dimensions of ourselves are much better defined and there is barely any further conflict among them.

What is feeling the inclination to love?

Having the liking and inclination to love is a way of being that develops from the soul or deep within. It is to be in the mood of feeling love and well disposed to reflect it. It is preliminary to being able to better love all that exists. We become famished to love. We feel swelled up inside without anything special happening in our lives. Nothing can quench our liking and inclination for loving and nothing can satisfy us. We never have enough of loving and all we want is to love... always and all the time. Once we have developed this inclination to love, all becomes a pretext to love... to love all that exists without exception. We experience enormous joy just by existing.

> *"Personally, I know few people who live this great joy on a continuous basis. They have transformed themselves enough to be able to love and live their lives this way. Their inclination and liking for loving has intensified itself and allows them to make their joy last and to love all that surrounds them. It is as if they had nothing left to ask God for themselves. Each time I have met them, they've seemed so happy, so relaxed and so comfortable. It is astonishing because they are happy, and only because of themselves, not because of external conditions."*

That is what is so marvelous! We can live this way with practice. Having the liking and inclination to love develops itself just like enlarging our scope for love and its rays. We surprise ourselves once we have surpassed our limits to love with more intensity; we love more things and more people.

This way of being becomes easy and natural because we remain connected with our soul which thrives on love only. For our soul to thrive on love only, we must learn a few spiritual lessons from what we live. We make our immature and hidden side evolve by going to the end of our illusions. We make the ego that is in our bodies and our chakras evolve to maturity. The ego is then replaced by light. In consequence, harmony will install itself and will reflect in our behaviors. Our inclination and liking to love is so strong that it transcends all that we are; then our love, the way it is in our soul, will manifest itself in a visible manner in our concrete world.

It is once we live our life that this way of being makes sense. If not, it would only be an unconfirmed concept or idea. It is by verifying with our material world that we see where all of this is leading us. We see the tangible results that it creates, because our soul inspires us to act, and we love all that exists much more and much better. We are amazed with this result because we come into a position to use our soul to neutralize all the disturbing energies that can create interferences and by what we are confronted with on the outside.

Others who see us are amazed by the changes in our behaviors because they themselves feel the peace that lives in us and that we also stimulate in them. They ask us questions because they want to know how we managed to change!

Where does the inclination to love come from?

The source that feeds our inclination to love is in fact ourselves. This source arouses our inner impulses that allow us to maintain our inclination for loving. It continuously pours in the appropriate energy which means that our liking and inclination to love will never dry up if we so choose . Once this source originates from ourselves, it can become inexhaustible. It does not depend on others or on any external circumstances.

If the source comes from others or the outside, it can dry up as fast as a puddle on a sunny day if circumstances change. In consequence, our liking and inclination for loving can disintegrate much easier which will incite us to stop loving.

For example, we often meet people who say they can no longer love after having fallen head over heals in love. Their inclination to love increased because of another person and their mind, which attributes and associates to this person the source of their inclination to love, blocks any attempts that could reanimate it. The end of their relationship means the end of their liking and inclination to love because the source has dried up.

The logic of the mind is very restrictive, and is not the point of view of the soul, who only wants to help us see clearer. We then realize that we can quench, by ourselves, our inclination to love without help from other people, and in whatever circumstances or conditions.

To see the limitations we have imposed on ourselves allows us to go further. We learn to surpass the limits of our beliefs that stop us from reaching a greater happiness. We learn to find new sources to our inclination to love in order to make it inexhaustible. These limits deprive us from the source that would feed our inclination for loving within ourselves. By becoming aware of it, we give ourselves access to love on a more lasting basis. We also give ourselves access to our soul.

What is love?

Love is a vibration and a happy feeling that comes from the soul. It is a miraculous energy that brings happiness where there is none.

Love is a feeling of joy that never ends!

It is a vibration that is so marvelous and becomes more sophisticated and subtle with time. As we live experiences, we learn to recognize it and we appreciate the well-being it brings.

Love is the strongest energy that exists on earth and it holds, in one form or another, the energies of all that exists in the physical world. If you want to understand what animates the physical world, look for it within yourself and in love, because it is there that you will find all the answers and no where else!

Love is a vibration that we feel. There is nothing else in fact, nothing but ourselves with our feelings. On the other hand, there is so much to say about the power of feeling love, of its impact and of all the attitudes it brings; the way of being and doing things, and also, how the others react to the love we reflect. The effect is an infinite multiplier because human beings need so much love... Or should I say, they need to feel so much unconditional love... the love that sleeps deep within their hearts and just awaits to burst out like a fountain. Once they feel it, they transform themselves and others around them, because love is like communicating vessels and there is no end.

The ones who need it the most are the ones who we refer to as destitute or criminals. Once they accept love or are stimulated to love, they transform themselves and become beings of love and light.

Love is whole, unique and indivisible.

Love is inseparable of all that exists because it forms one body within it. From its essence, it is unconditional and it includes the full and complete acceptance of others for who and what they are, as well as the full acceptance of all that happens, as it happens.

We only love, and the right to exist, in all that has been created, is legitimate. All that exists is fully given the freedom to be who and what it is, and we only love it without wanting to possess it. We desire happiness for others and we wish it ardently without having any expectations.

To separate love, divide it, or make it conditional means depriving oneself from further benefits and limiting happiness... One is then making love what it is not, to begin learning and understanding what love really is.

Once love is in our soul, it is unconditional. It could be transformed into conditional love by the individual before it is reflected in the visible world. However, it then loses its deep sense and can even be grasped and recuperated by our mind that makes it an objective, while it is a state of being.

Love does not begin in our mind, but in our souls. It is not a project constructed in our mind or by our mind to obtain or attract love from the outside. We do not try to provoke love for ourselves, from our spouse, our children or any other person by loving them, because that is what we call a love project created by our minds. It is our mind that plans love for our heart in order to achieve its own goals.

This love that takes root in our soul and at the source of all life is very different from the mental love that is created and that lives in our minds only. Then, love installs itself everywhere in ourselves, in all our visible or invisible dimensions, and in our deepest and hidden dimensions. It is only vibrations and feelings that are not situated on the plane of ideas or concepts. It leaves our soul and extends to all what we are.

Once love becomes intense, it might also reach our unconsciousness.

We also feel love and a great peacefulness when we dream at night because the conflicts within ourselves are a story of the past. It's as if joy overcomes us day and night! Since we feel good and are no longer afraid, we no longer have nightmare, because a nightmare is feeling fear to attract fear. It is an indication that love has not yet reached and taken root in all our dimensions, and that there is still room for improvement and fulfillment in some of them.

When we feel our love intensely, we tame fear on a conscious level. Because of its intensity, our love shines and this shining is perceived concretely in all our components. It also happens in our unconscious zones where peace has also rooted and installed itself. Our lives become easier to live because love is present everywhere and in every aspect of our dimensions.

Is fun a part of love and happiness?

Fun, as we describe it from the human point of view or as we live it in human passions is not an obligatory condition for happiness, even though it can be associated with it. Human passions do not need to all be satisfied in order to feel fun or happiness, or to be able to love. Love contains all within itself; all that the human being needs to be happily satisfied and completely fed with all he can imagine or need on the psychological plane.

Love holds a great power of happiness, an enormous potential that can incite any individual to as much fun as any human can live. This fun is different from the fun we were used to in human passions. It is not well known but just as real and as intense!

We acquire the inclination for liking fun and we have good dispositions to play, if we have not yet developed them, but without depending on them to be happy. We also do not depend on the outside world to experience them and to be satisfied. This inclination for playing or for laughter represents positive outcomes of our liking and inclination to love that we can express in a visible manner when the opportunity occurs. We do not depend on expressing it in the outside world to feel happiness. We are self-sufficient the way we are, whether or not we express it. We accept any external event the way it happens.

An inclination to love that is intensified can neutralize all our worries.

Sometimes, our indication and impetus for loving is so strong that it takes up all the room. We are in a state of semi-contemplation towards all that exists. We feel a kind of ecstasy and grace that pushes us to thank God for all we are living and all that exists.

We know how to neutralize any energy that could spoil our happiness. It is with confidence that we take on the small problems of life. We place all of our worries and problems in the hands of God and we peacefully accept all that will happen. In the meantime, we continue loving and never cease feeling it.

We make ourselves available to happiness by putting aside all of our problems to simply continue loving as if nothing ever happened. Of course, we solve them, but only when the time comes to do so. We then take action, but in a way so simple as if the time has finally come to perform a very familiar routine, like brushing our teeth or combing our hair. The problem is still there, but without the worries that usually accompany it. Our happiness has overcome all the compulsions and the constraints created by the physical world and let me tell you, my dear friends, that we are all able to perform such marvels.

The happiness of loving contains all the joys that the material world could bring us.

Our liking and inclination for amusement, laughter and fun join together and merge into a new kind of feeling that contains all of them at the same time. The reason is that the bliss which comes from loving with our soul provides us with such a great feeling, an ecstatic happiness that brings us all the good fortunes, benefits and satisfaction that they could otherwise bring, if we use the outside world as a vehicle to live them. We feel a satisfaction that is close to maximum fulfillment.

Experiencing this feeling is so simple, because we only need ourselves to live it and we don't need any outside support. We no longer depend on the material world to live them and our inner impulses that pushed us merge together in a marvelous and delightful sensual pleasure, in a bliss that the outside and the material world could never equal.

They could never make us feel it with such intensity. Nothing as exciting! It couldn't be any other way because we contribute to it with every aspect of ourselves, our human and divine aspects, to recreate the happiness we feel.

> *"I, Gilles, want to testify that I am able to live such intense happiness on this earth. Living on earth becomes like living in paradise. We are fulfilled and we stop dreaming about what else we would need to be happy. We feel a deep and strong happiness and we are satisfied with it! We just appreciate how we are and what we possess as it is."*

We have a strong inclination for happiness and we feel light. Once we have this liking for happiness, we use all that is in the outside world as a pretext to feel it more. We can testify in the material world and demonstrate by our concrete actions all the inner delight we live. Our behaviors reflect it and we invite everyone who needs it to nourish from it. We are ready to share the best of ourselves with them, and we welcome them with a smile.

Imprisoning happiness in material things limits our access to a greater happiness and to the bliss.

Once we depend only on the physical world to live happy feelings, it becomes rare that we can use all our capabilities at the same time to make ourselves happy.

This is how we limit ourselves. We often remain unsatisfied and it's the material world that limits us, like we limit ourselves from within. The material things and the physical world are parts of what we call the finite. So the happiness becomes boxed up. Since I have a small house, my happiness can only be small. But if I had the big house I've always dreamed of, then I could feel a grand happiness. Why limit ourselves this way? The invisible Universe and the inner realities have no limits and the happiness we discover is unlimited.

Some people also imprison beauty in physical forms, and pleasure in physiological feelings which they feel when they come in contact with others. All this will limit their access to a serene and delightful life. All of this makes it more difficult to attain lasting happiness, pleasure and joy while living our lives.

Having the inclination to love, loving, learning to love and experiencing love are all different!

It is a pleasure to share with you what we know on this topic.

Each individual continuously tries and wants to develop his inclination to love and to feel it, without even being conscious of it and without knowing how to achieve it. By increasing his liking and inclination to love, each individual looks for more happiness because that is its reason for being. Everyone realizes at one point in time that hating is not relaxing or easy to live through.

Our intuition tells us that hating pushes away peace and happiness. It is not satisfying because the human being is fundamentally made and conceived to love. It is his deep nature because loving makes him happy; which means the more he will love without condition, the happier he will be.

Once we have developed the liking and inclination to love and we really feel it, we stop wanting to change others. We love them for who and what they are. We just want to love them and are not only content; we are delighted with it. If we have not developed the inclination to love, we try to be in a better position to acquire it by changing others to enable us to love them in a way that is consistent with our own criteria. We can then develop our inclination and liking to love, because we don't know yet how to love and we feel the need to have this inclination. What pushes us is the intuition that loving will bring us peace and happiness.

Once our liking and inclination for love becomes intense enough, all that surrounds us becomes lovable by itself, just as it is. It acquires the right to be loved by us. It is as we have given to each thing the property of being lovable. In fact, our love only rebounds to the outside like a gigantic fountain that falls on all that exists. The sun doesn't shine for only a few flowers. It shines for all that exists. It is the same for our heart which is somewhat like the sun.

Every human being seeks only happiness at all times.

Behind all kinds of appearances that take on numerous forms, every individual, in fact, seeks a lasting happiness. But it doesn't always seem to be the case. If we take a good look, we would see that each individual always does the best he can do to be happy with the conscience level he has reached at any particular moment of his life. He seeks to understand what he is living to make it. He experiences different situations by trial and error. He often makes mistakes before understanding how to be happy and what to do to reach this goal. He often needs to explore the disillusions that "non-loving" brings, before he can understand what love is. It is then that he can finally manage his life better.

This is why every individual deserves compassion and love at all times. This is why God always loves him. He always deserves that we continue to love and help him, no matter what he says or does. He is always worthy of mercy! He always deserves a last chance, because it is never too late to improve. He often doesn't know any better, even when it doesn't appear to be the case.

After numerous attempts to become happier by various means, we begin to realize that true happiness cannot be reached if we are incapable of loving. The criminal and the assassin are confronted with learning it by means of great suffering. They will pay a hefty price just to enjoy a few small moments of pleasure or excitement. Let's stop hating them in order to understand how great their distress and suffering could be. Their importance is related to the type of illusions they materialize. All they do to others will one day happen to them, and this will continue until they realize that the true sense of their life is to feel and demonstrate love. We can escape the human laws, but we can never escape the universal laws; the laws of God.

How can we be happy?

By developing our aptitudes and capabilities of happiness and by learning to love all that exists... By this, nothing can disturb the feelings of joy and peace that live in us. Loving all that exists guarantees that all surrounding us or which happens to us will always make us happy.

Hiding behind mountains of material wealth will fail to protect us from unhappiness, misfortune and trouble. Sooner or later, unhappiness will catch up, because, within ourselves, there remains the magnet and the force of attraction for unhappiness to manifest itself in our life, and this is what we truly need to change.

Happiness is tamable and we attract it to us to make it a faithful friend. This is done in stages. Our happiness is built step by step, slowly but surely on the basis of knowing ourselves a little more each day. Each day that goes by, we learn to love ourselves more and more. We learn to love all that exists with more fervor and more flexibility. We go through adjustment periods where our illusions and beliefs are put to the test facing the reality that we create in order for us to evolve and grow.

We confront ourselves more each day to discover new facets of our identity. These discoveries increase the knowledge of our reality and widen our zone of conscience. We push back our unconsciousness and we transform our ego to learn to constantly love a little bit better. We keep learning more about what to do to make ourselves happy. There is no end, only marvelous challenges that renew themselves each day. As is the law of evolution, a law that can create such hope in the heart of the human being that will admit his existence.

Loving is a preliminary condition to permanent happiness and to this day, we have never met anyone who could live an intense and permanent happiness without being capable of loving.

Does love bring suffering?

Then, why do certain people claim to suffer from loving?... Why do they suffer?...

Well, here is a plausible explanation! It is simply because they still need to learn how to love and because they still don't know enough about it. They don't know how to intensify their love, making it unconditional and thus avoid all suffering. What provokes suffering is not love, but the lack of knowledge which although it has not yet been achieved and learned, is now on the right track. We do not suffer in vain, because, each time we learn new things about ourselves. We discover new facets.

We never suffer from love or because we love too much. On the contrary! If we suffer, it is because we couldn't love enough or because we don't love as we should or, again, because we love in the wrong way. What we will discover at the end is that we don't love ourselves enough or we love ourselves the wrong way, and that produces the suffering.

We can give the love we feel a deeper sense, make it more divine and sublime. Loving without conditions will never bring suffering. It is when we add conditions to love or when our mind interferes that suffering manifests and appears.

We still need to learn to love in order to stop projecting on others what we will eventually find within ourselves. Because, we compensate for our shortcomings by projecting upon others that which actually relates to the work on ourselves we have not done yet. Love, brought back to a very human level, loses its divine essence and its power to create happiness. The human being is totally capable of preserving its divine and unconditional character. By doing so, he can continue to invent his joy and to always create it with more skills and awareness at all times.

By harmonizing all our dimensions, we can love all that exists without suffering.

We love because we want to be happy and both, love and happiness, occur often at the same time. We feel the need to love more and more once our liking or inclination to love is intensified. Loving can often be summarized by achieving these motivations. The other motivations that would push us to love come from the illusions of loving created by our mind that makes us believe that we love. In actuality, we are only indicating our preferences from a human point of view when we separate what is lovable and what isn't. This is different from loving together with your heart and your soul which is more global and embraces all that exists, in every aspect.

Loving by excluding certain aspects of ourselves creates both disharmonies and suffering. Harmony comes by accepting all aspects of our dimensions and by making them work all together in a complementary relationship to attain the common goal: the goal of loving! This goal is reached when unconditional love becomes a rock-solid structure and foundation of living, a concrete result that is visible in the physical world.

If we get hurt by loving, it is because we don't know yet how to love. We need to learn it with all our dimensions to attain harmony and integrate love within all ourselves, not just certain selected components. We need to integrate it in all that we are to fully reflect it in all that we do. If we fully understood how to love, it wouldn't hurt. The more we are hurt by loving, the greater our need for learning how to love grows.

Learning to love at times may mean that we need to experience "non-loving" or loving with our mind only, to see just how far and where it will lead us. We may experience this painful apprenticeship in the physical world for the greater purpose of realizing our mind's limitations and the little satisfaction that this kind of loving brings.

Afterwards, there is a good chance we will be in a better position to love with our soul by putting into gear all the components of ourselves that we can possibly use as a harmonized whole.

What is experiencing love?

It is to reflect the vibrations and sensations of joy coming from our soul with all our behaviors in order to achieve and realize all of love's benefits. Before we do this, we must first have recreated a definite harmony in our bodies (physical, emotional, mental and energetic) and our chakras. We must also have gained a certain awareness; having integrated the spiritual reality in order to be able to understand: what love is as it exists in our soul?... That is to know: what is merely mental love?... what truly is, loving?...

How can we transpose our liking and inclination to love to the outside?... How can we reflect love into the material world exactly as it exists in our soul?... Some even need to experience hate in order to be able to love with more purity and clearness.

In other words, to experience love as it is in our soul, we must first create definite conditions that allow us to truly reflect it into the physical world. We often mistake the experiencing of love for the process of learning to love, which is the acquisition of the abilities that allow us to love more with our soul and purposely recreate the appropriate conditions to do it time and again. These two aspects of loving usually happen at the same time, because once we experience love, we learn to love more, and the effect is retroactive on our abilities to love. The opposite however is not always true. There is often a gap before we actually feel love. At the time we learn loving, the process has to follow its due course before love itself can be present and for us to feel the benefits of the lesson.

By experiencing love, we further harmonize our bodies and our chakras. The beneficial effect has no end. We increase our awareness and, by the same token, we increase our abilities to love. Since we never stop learning, we reflect it better and better just as it is in our soul. We do it more and more each day that goes by and consequently we love better and better.

We only learn to love and enlarge our awareness, and this is why each individual is on earth. We are always learning with a few or several of our dimensions at the same time.

The outside is only the reflection of ourselves for learning to love.

What motivated the incarnation of any human being is grandiose and we recognize there, the presence of God in all his goodness and the intention of the soul to evolve more.

At the end, if we have problems loving others, we can always feel in our heart how each individual fits into the vast plan of God and why he as an individual, is on earth. For example, why is the criminal here? If God gave him his chance to learn like all others, then, why do we have the tendency to push him aside and reject him? Irremediably condemning him as bad? Let's look for the answer within ourselves and discover why we don't believe and forget that he too could learn and better himself one day! I am willing to bet you that this is not the vision of God! You see, the criminal then wouldn't be on this earth learning like the rest of us to begin with, would he now?

Why do certain persons cross our paths or remain present in our thoughts? Aren't they there as a reflection of certain aspects of ourselves... To be used by us as a foundation for becoming aware of certain dimensions that we are learning to love or that we need to change and make more room for yet more love? This is the only reason that these thoughts are present in our zone of conscience.

What strikes you about any particular individual could be considered as something you need to change in yourself right now! Being him is like being you and what strikes a chord with you from him are only the aspects of yourself that hold messages which you have to learn, to grasp, and decode, in order to arrive at a position to love yourself more, now! It is now that this in particular needs to happen and not tomorrow, because tomorrow, your needs will be different and you will become aware of yet other things. What happens now is what we need now, and this relevancy is always maintained. It is why we need right now to decode the messages that others send us and to see them as information regarding ourselves.

Others show us what needs to be changed within ourselves.

This justifies and explains what has just reached our consciousness regarding others and why, for now and all time, there is no one but ourselves left to learn how to love on our own. It all comes down to this and we often refuse to face ourselves. We refuse to see ourselves as we are within others, even if they demonstrate it to us many times before we accept the truth. Others through their behaviors take the responsibility of reminding us. They have this marvelous mandate, just as we have towards them, because each and every one of us are enrolled in this vast plan of God, this vast plan of progress towards light and love.

Facing the challenges that we encounter, God gave each of us, at least the minimum capabilities to be able to overcome them. It is why we feel that he is infinitely good. If you encounter many barriers that could stop you from reflecting love at all times, realize that you have even more abilities within yourself that can allow you to eliminate them. Look within you and you will be amazed to find the gold mine that you have never discovered in others.

There is nothing on the outside that can stop us from progressing on our road towards light. We can consider the obstacles we encounter as challenges that reinforce our determination to learn. Thank God to provide us with the opportunity to prove ourselves.

Liking to learn obliges peaceful contemplation and humility.

Liking to learn is part of loving without conditions, because we like the challenges our own imperfections and difficult situations bring. These are perfect opportunities to verify our aptitudes to love and to become more aware of what level our inclination and liking to love have reached. Since we only want to learn, without judging ourselves, we accept with serenity what our limits are and we take note of them.

When we look at them from this point of view, the difficult situations which we live through lose a lot of their importance. They become as common as the routine ones. They also lose their negative and undesirable aspects. The same thing occurs when we discover new faults or new imperfections about ourselves. It is then much easier to fully accept them and grant them acceptable values, values equivalent to our qualities or to the aspects of ourselves we consider more perfect.

Once we have learned to love, all what we have to do has far less importance, as it is all placed on the same ground. It is the case for taking on any new challenge, doing what we like to do or what we have already done with brilliance. All that happens has almost the same level of importance; we accept each situation as it comes, with peace, to simply live it without asking so many questions and without worrying. Our mind takes a break and rests and our heart puts all that we live in the hand of God. We no longer separate what is undesirable from what is desirable, because we have learned to put them all on the same ground and come to the place we do it naturally.

We appreciate any situation for what it contains in beauty and usefulness. We accept and appreciate life as it is, without wasting our time thinking if the weather will be nice tomorrow, or trying to find out what the future holds for us. We take great pleasure in enjoying and feeling life and that's all! In this way, we learn to master and go beyond any fear or anguish.

Accepting all that happens with peace can be learned!

Instead of refusing what happens to us, we accept it peacefully. Since we are sincere towards ourselves, we can globally accept all the aspects of our being and all what we are. And just because of that, we can also accept all that happens in the same way and with a similar attitude. Since we fully accept ourselves in the way we experience all that happens, there is no more room for anguish and fear which are immediately replaced with peace and calm.

All that happens to us and all what we live for are linked to what we are. By accepting ourselves better, we can more easily accept what happens to us. We develop the liking and the inclination for unconditional acceptance, abandonment and detachment. No fear can resist as it all vanishes. When we have developed a strong inclination to love and that this inclination comes from our soul, we accept all that can happen, even our physical disharmonies or diseases. All physical problems now represent new learning opportunities about and for ourselves. Right away, we accept them as a means to further explore ourselves on our own.

We realize, once again, all the goodness of God through what we live, because we always have the time to react in order to change that has created the problem and to better live in what happens. We could even become in more pitiful condition before realizing it.

> *"We have our qualms just like you, but it will not prevent us from loving, because nothing can diminish our love. Nothing can take away our appreciation for life, even if our imperfections meet the eye. With love, I make the unbearable bearable and I tame what is frightful.*
>
> *Once the physical suffering arouses in my body, the margin of difficulty also grows, but I can only feel better by finding and looking at the good side of this situation... Because there is always a bright side!"*

It is what we know and this awareness motivates us to remain positive and to continue feeling love. We can reach deeper within ourselves to feel and discover why all this is happening. We use our peace of mind to calm the physical annoyances, may they be small or big. The uncomfortable becomes more comfortable. The strength of our love can determine our limits in this matter.

Globally accepting all of our dimensions allows us to live with serenity all that happens.

Once we become aware of what we have already accomplished, we extend it to other zones of ourselves. Therefore, our faults and imperfections become equivalent to the other aspects of ourselves that are more perfect. Our faults and our qualities are put on the same level and we accept them both as a simple reality, without judgment of values. It is an existing reality which we accept and face, visualizing with detachment; we even look at all of it with some indifference whether it is a quality, a fault, or a physical disharmony, we accept it without dramatizing. We use the same logic for difficult or easy situations, for good fortune or misfortune, they all have a bright and good side that we value by continuing to love.

At all times and in any circumstance, we only want to better ourselves and to correct our faults without ever depreciating ourselves for as little as one of our faults. Whether we fail or succeed, it makes no difference and is no longer important, because we will still love ourselves no matter what! Intense love always triumphs! There are no more true defeats, only victories! This is the miracle of love, its magic that dazzles us...

This situation occurs when we have learned to love and have mastered the art of loving. All we do is love because our inclination and liking to love is so intense! We love all that exists and all is a pretext to continue loving and not cease doing so. Our faults as well as any undesirable situation that arises cannot escape this rule. This way, we can maintain, at all times, happiness in our heart. It is what we look for and it is also what you are seeking. It is also our soul's wish.

> *"Seeing the good side of my imperfections is what I call loving myself a little bit more... My love becomes more complete and more global...This is how the imperfection is perfect, because it will always help us learn something... Learn to accept ourselves without conditions. Any human being will see its use if he takes the time to look at it from a spiritual point of view."*

Loving is no mystery!

Without exception, we are all able to love! We can all learn how to love better, and that never stops and never ends. This is especially true for the ones who think and believe they are already capable of loving. They often have a tendency of falling back to what they have already learned.

Because they have already loved and are capable of loving, certain people think they have sufficiently mastered the art of loving! By congealing as such, they only prepare themselves to learn to love more by integrating further what they already know. Adjustments are often needed to be able to love more and better. As these adjustments are made, they will then lose other antiquated or false beliefs about love, which will allow them to feel love more by returning to their soul to feel it and appreciate even more it at this level.

Congealing evolution is a mental process that means that they are no longer situated at the level of their soul to love. It's only a question of time before they realize they can still learn to love. Once we realize we still have learning to do, we start a new lesson because we manifest humility and have already opened the door for a grander apprenticeship to happen in our life.

To love with more ease, we all have a large and beautiful heart which can be opened further, when necessary. Concrete and practical exercises exist to achieve this.

Starting right now, you can open and reinforce the chakra of your heart

There are many techniques that can teach you how to open the chakra of your heart and purify it in order to be capable of loving without condition and loving more; how to inspire energy at the level of your heart by using the chakras; how to stimulate the chakra of your heart with hands or with words, because these specific actions can be directed where the needs are located at the heart's level.

Each individual can capture energy from the beyond or from the angels with his coronal chakra. This energy and the light can be redirected toward the dysfunctional chakra of the heart or directly to the heart of any other person. By using the chakras of our hands which are connected to the chakra of our heart, we can directly intervene on the hearts of the others or stimulate their chakras of the heart. This would certainly help them to channel love better and maintain it more in their hearts. We can also use our frontal chakra, where the conscience sits, to increase the effect on the heart. This experience can be repeated as necessary. The opening of the heart can be created this way and it is the beginning of a beautiful love story that can make more than one person cry!

With practice, we learn to keep our heart open!

By verifying how we are in our actions, and by practicing to continue loving when nothing incites us, we can learn to keep our heart open all the time, which completes the technical work we might have already benefited from.

Thus, we develop confidence; the confidence that all that will happen is for the best; the confidence that we can dominate our ordeals and burdens and continue to love and be happy. We are confident that after the rain, there is sunshine, and that there is always a greater happiness waiting for us.

We help ourselves and that is loving and loving ourselves... Taking charge of our life to take care of ourselves!... If we don't do it, who will? Who can love us better than ourselves?... No one can do it better than we can!... In action, we increase our awareness and we always integrate love deeper within ourselves! We strengthen the chakra of our heart and we enrich our love significantly.

What is the use of being helped by others to open our heart, if we don't do anything ourselves to keep it open afterwards? We are the only ones who can develop our aptitude to love and reinforce our confidence in life! No one can do it for us!

We can all develop our aptitudes to love!

The power of a heart and its aptitude to love is measured by its capacity to stay open when everything urges it to close up! The real test and burdens occur when abuse of trust and hard shots keep occurring and hurting... For example, having been "stabbed in the back", being lied to or being a victim of cheating or any flagrant injustice. Here you have all it takes to feel like a victim!... It all justifies closure, but we choose to keep our heart open.

How can we reach this stage and maintain it? It is through our trust or confidence in life; it throws our solid foundations in front of the ordeals and continues to maintain our love, because our inclination to love and our love are too intense for our heart to close up. A heart that strictly holds conditional or human love will close up, but the heart that is fed by and swims in divine and unconditional love will stay open.

It's the soul that feeds divine love to the heart, and the richness of a heart well fed is demonstrated with facts. A well experienced heart masters the art of loving. It is able to stay open at all times, when nothing urges it to do so on the outside.

We surpass the beliefs and the mental resolutions that tell us we will not be caught again in such a difficult situation and that the best solution would be to close up in order to protect ourselves! After a few experiences where all solutions come from our mind, we open up to our heart to live emotions of compassion and confidence, instead of taking refuge in our mind which often is in a state of alarm. The mind wants to mobilize all of our organism into a state of panic, facing the fear of suffering.

First of all, we can reassure our minds, because we now know that behind each suffering, there is always new happiness hiding, only awaiting the opportunity to grow! Doing this, we significantly reduce the activity of the mind and its disproportionate influence, because we have realized that it is not as useful as other dimensions of ourselves are in bringing us peace in such circumstances.

Even when undergoing hardships, we can still keep our heart open and continue to love.

Because our conscience brings us a larger view, we realize that the vision of our mind is limited by what is logical and understood with reason. We surpass that and go beyond because we know with our heart and soul that there is so much joy in loving, and there always will be this deep contentment. Since we know this is so, why close our hearts and ourselves out from love?... Instead of closing up, we open! We open more towards ourselves, to listen and hear ourselves crying with tenderness, and when facing grief, we feel sympathy towards ourselves.

Instead of escaping, we are able to stay in our heart when the crisis intensifies its sharpness. We only look at ourselves with love and compassion. The boat could tip but we refuse to leave it, or desert it! We stay in place and watch the agitated sea with peace knowing that the nice weather and calm will resume again soon. We continue to have confidence in life, that life will still have pleasant surprises for us. We can already feel and imagine it! This helps us feel better.

By opening ourselves to our heart, we can keep it open. Our conscience, that we have already linked to our soul, allows us to neutralize all the hardships we face with love, which will dissolve them and always rise with triumph!

Once peace has been established we spread to each and every part of our physical body the well-being that we feel in our heart. It is actually in the entire physical dimension of our being that all the troubles we have experienced have taken place. So, it is also throughout our whole physical body that this integration materializes itself, and this becomes concrete, when our generalized well-being increases everywhere within ourselves.

A strong inclination to love can resist any storm!

Facing all the abuse we go through, we fall back on all that is beautiful within ourselves to appreciate and love it. By recharging our batteries this way, we can always bounce back stronger and stronger. This happens in the frame of a grand opening to ourselves. This is sufficient to keep our heart open because loving ourselves holds in itself all we need to be happy. We need to feel this and develop the ability by practicing it and by maintaining our confidence in life. We then feel compassion for the abuser. It is naturally and without forcing ourselves that we wish love and light for his heart that may be suffering or half closed.

"I Gilles, can no longer prevent myself from loving!... Loving all who have been abusing me; the ones who let me down, or could still break my heart, because it is without difficulty that my liking or inclination to love extends itself to them and to all who could still incite me to close up my heart. I look towards God with trust to draw the strength to continue. I choose to continue to love because I want to continue to be happy. Since I have

been through such situations, I have realized that I could continue to love at all times!

My inclination to love is like a hurricane inside me, and it is like I have electricity in my whole body, loving with 10,000 volts. Who can stop the current from going through?... It is with joy and gratitude that I love all who incite me to close up my heart. They have taught me to love at all times and in any circumstance. They represent a marvelous challenge, a challenge that I needed to verify my abilities and to become aware of my aptitudes to keep my heart open!"

We need discover the extent to which we can continue to love when others incite us to do the opposite. To what extent can we go?... We realize at what stage we are in our capabilities to love. Certain beliefs then have a lot to ingest or no longer hold. We stop thinking we are good, to simply be good or simply recognize that we still have a lot to learn about ourselves, if we want to be good or improve ourselves.

Others help us by showing us the limits of our love.

Others who incite us to hate or close up our heart show us to what extent we are able to love at all times, in all places and in any circumstances. Let's stop judging, and let's face ourselves and see in others who demonstrate to us where we are in the stages of our aptitudes to love.

We should consider the behavior of others like a movie about ourselves that we can see through the eyes of our soul. It's like going to the cinema! We can see what we become, because their life is like a screen where we reflect ourselves as actors in the role we have chosen to play.

Let's have the humility to see ourselves as we truly are and the courage to start where we stand to build with ourselves on solid ground. Let us stop looking for mental excuses to justify the closure of our heart! Let's simply admit that we don't exactly know how to draw from our souls all the liking and inclination to love we need to love further and under any condition.

Let's bring back our confidence in life. Losing confidence and regaining it is merely a process that consists of building the confidence and trust that can and will resist any ordeal. This is how I, Gilles, have acquired an indestructible confidence in life.

Can we feel love at all times?

Can we feel love no matter what happens? Now there is a guideline that orientates us toward what needs to be changed within ourselves to have the inclination to love and act with love. Because having the liking and inclination to love and feeling this as a need is an extraordinary stimulus that nothing can stop. Nothing will stop you from loving all that exists at all times if you push to the extreme your liking and inclination to love.

This comes fast, and rises rapidly from your soul to your heart, from your heart to your conscience and from your conscience to your physical body and from your entire body to the exterior to conclude itself in the form of behaviors filled with softness and kindness. You will have eyes of compassion and tenderness. All your gestures will demonstrate your deep kindness and will harmonize with so much goodness that will reflect in all the actions you take.

Let's go further than our primary reactions and demonstrate to everyone that we are still capable to love even if nothing is urging us to.

> *"Today, I can affirm that I was already able to keep my heart open even when undergoing contrary pressures. Nothing and no one can urge me to close it because I know to what extent we can be happy by keeping our heart open. It is in the face of everyone that I say it and it is with humility ,simplicity and naiveté that I invite you to observe me if you want to know how I managed to do so. You can all do like me if you want to, because I am no better than you, no more skillful or more clever, I am just like you with the courage to take myself on hand!"*

You are all capable of keeping your heart open!

It is with joy that I proclaim this! You all have a heart and soul to love just as I do! Your heart is capable of large transformations and your love, once intensified, could even become miraculous!

It is with great respect that I want to give you the truth and "the right time," because you all deserve love and happiness. You all deserve to live a permanent and lasting happiness, simply because you exist; all simply because your souls are all of an immense beauty; and because of their potential for light and divinity that they could always reflect in a visible way. I see this beauty pouring through all you are and simply looking at you now brings me a lot of joy!

Human life makes sense, once we are able to look at all that exists with love. Anything that exists and all that we become aware of is considered to be a friend who has come along just to help us.

We discover this friendly link with anything or anyone, once we turn toward ourselves to find the thread that reunited us. A circuit of energy is then created in both directions and peace moves into our heart in a sort of amazement and plenitude of being.

"It is what I call 'reconciliating' with the material world. Seeing God in it allows us to love all these material things without attachment. This presence of God in all things allows us to create a link of love with all that exists, because God is also in our heart and we can reunite the divine energy. First of all, we project with our conscience and our third eye a beam of light and energy that weaves a link of harmony with all that exists or all we see.

The divine energy merges into an invisible whole at the level of our heart where we put a seal from the happiness we feel."

CHAPTER II EXERCISES

1. RE-PROGRAMMING OF THE SUBCONSCIOUS

One way to re-program your subconscious regarding your beliefs on love is through positive affirmations. By repeating them with ardor, and by accompanying them with emotions and feelings that they arouse in you, you will change rapidly. It is important to practice regularly, since it is only a question of time before you transform your states of being. Your mental and emotional dimensions will be encouraged to undergo important transformations, which will bring about other changes in your other dimensions and your entire being.

TRANSFORMATION OF YOUR BELIEFS ON LOVE

"I feel the great happiness that my heart produces by loving. Nothing can spoil the happiness I feel right now. I have once felt this great joy, and I have made it mine.

I am no longer questioning myself about it. It is all over now! I love and I know that my love is a vibration, a feeling that brings everlasting joy. I feel love, with pleasure and ecstasy. I feel it endlessly.

My unconscious knows it as well as my conscious and there is no more room for doubts left in my mind. My subconscious has fully accepted it as my new reality. I have already accepted the fact that the love I feel derives from me and that I represent its unique source.

I know that the others are not the source of my love, since it is me, and only me that produces it. The love I feel resides in me, in my own heart and not in the hearts of other people. I have chosen not to let anyone lessen my inclination and liking to love that have risen from my soul. I have chosen to love and to keep my heart open at all times. Now, I always keep my heart open, because I feel that it is good to love.

I have recovered my power to love and the others only serve as a pretext to show my love. I love with my heart and, tomorrow, I will love in the same manner, and with as much intensity!"

We suggest you to read this text at least three times a day, while allowing its energy to enfold you. Read it in the morning at home, in the middle of the day at your place of work, and in the evening. Do this during three months and be alert to observe the changes that will take place in the way you feel.

Be watchful of the vibrations that will emanate from your heart, and how you will react to burdens and pitfalls that life could bring you.

There will be changes following this exercise, because you are calling forth the higher dimensions of yourself that govern your life, and you supply them with new tools to help you. These tools will allow love to take a bigger place in the solutions to the problems you will meet.

The solutions will rather be found in your "being" (how you are) instead of in your "doing" (what you do). In changing your ways of being, you re-invent your life with more originality and imagination. You create with more light and with a greater radiance that install themselves in your soul.

2. HEALING OF THE HEART
1st STEP: CONTACT THE EVENT

Look back at the events in your life where you felt heartbroken. For example: the breakdown of an intimate relationship, loss of a loved one, betrayal, arguments, etc...

- Realize how you have lived these events by living them again, exactly as they have then occurred.

- Now, get in touch with one of those events. What was the level of your conscience at that time?

- Contact your ego during that event, the ego you rely on to live it. What role did it play?

- Take an honest look at yourself at that time. Identify and point out your ways of being and doing things that you have shown during that event. Is there more room for love and light? Remember that if you carry wounds due to this event, it is because it has been experienced with a certain lack of consciousness, wisdom and maturity. Otherwise, it would not have left such a painful reminder.

2nd STEP: COMPARE WITH TODAY

- Compare with what you know now, with the additional knowledge you have gained to this day. In other words, how would you relive this event today?

- Compare with your present conscience and use your new ways of being to relive the event.

- Relive the same event using your conscience of today in order to bring into it more love and light.

- Look at yourself through the eyes of compassion, and accept your errors for what they are, because they have fed your learning process and they have been useful. Without them, you would not be who you are today, and you would not have raised as much to your level of consciousness. Without them, you would not have access to the new ways of being which you are now able of creating to bring you back to a state of joy. Without them, you would not have been able to learn to love as well as you do today.

- Allow yourself to feel thoroughly the emotions that arise from this event, without suppressing, choking or blocking them.

- Feel their non-love, their immaturity and their lack of consciousness if it is the case.

- Once you have become impregnated with all the emotions and feelings related to this event, go on to the next exercise which will help you to transcend the pain.

3rd STEP: TRANSCEND THE PAIN

- Join your hands together at your waist level. With your palms facing up, imagine this problem resting in your hands. Raise your arms and hand your problem over to the Universe, the Beyond or to God who will take care of it. Surrender to them all that you have experienced, all your attitudes, feelings and emotions connected to this particular event.

- Feel the peace growing inside of you, as you surrender and let go of your pain and your sorrow to the higher forces.

- Start over three times and repeat out loud: *"I give up, I surrender, and I let go these problems and suffering; I now leave!"*

- Feel the usefulness of the event you have lived and surround with love, everything that has occurred.

- Ask for help from your soul and your spirit guides and realize all that your soul has learned due to that event.

- Let your trust and confidence be known to your soul for the experience it has chosen for you... Confidence and trust that were shaken up, but that you are now taking back and re-affirming with more intensity.

4th STEP: CHANGE WHAT YOU HAVE LIVED

With your present thoughts and emotions, relive this event another time, and, this time, by using your conscience, change the way you have experienced it. Live it the way that will provide you with a greater satisfaction. Forget what happened in the past.

- Change the course of what happened by using love and confidence... Confidence that whatever happened in the past was for the best.

- Add more light into the event and relive it the way you would have wanted to live it, while respecting yourself and loving what you choose.

- Affirm that it is what you are changing now that will remain engraved in your heart and in your soul.

- Visualize that your heart is bathing in a blue-golden light, and feel that this healing energy is permeating it more and more.

Your thoughts and emotions change what was once imprinted in your soul and in your heart, and you are now moving forward from a new basis. As you program your heart to love, your emotional body enlarges its zone of love and the non-love diminishes.

These four steps allow you to:

TRANSCEND YOUR EGO
TO REACH THE LOVE IN YOUR HEART!...
THIS SOURCE ONLY AWAITS YOUR SIGNAL
TO BURST OUT!

- Start over the entire exercise (the four steps), using another event.

- Review each event until there are none left to heal.

"Heal your heart and your soul, and let the Paradise to materialize in your life!"

CHAPTER III

What Is Good About Loving?

LOVING IS USEFUL FOR SO MANY THINGS!

Loving is useful, especially to live our life in joy because true love is inseparable from happiness. Loving is also useful in feeling tenderness, well-being and the peace that it brings, because we also need it to live. Loving is used to receive and welcome these feelings that we choose to give ourselves, exactly in the same way as if they came from others.

There are no more differences... Reconciliation happens between the different dimensions of ourselves, which leads to the fusion of feelings we arouse in ourselves by using others as a pretext to make it and the feelings we arouse on our own without going through others.

True love includes the divine love and unconditional love that we have learned to feel for all that exists. If human love seems inhuman to you sometimes, and brings suffering, the divine love on the other hand, is always adequate for the human being and always ends with a sense of well-being and joy! It never brings misfortune. It only nourishes the good sides of life and always brings all that we need to be happy.

Human love ends with the end of the physical body and human life, but divine love goes on. It never dies or ends because it continues its trip with the soul. It transcends age, time and space. Developing it on earth assures a beautiful and shining continuity in the beyond.

The divine love we experience on earth prepares our future routes towards what we will orientate ourselves to in the spiritual world; what we choose now to live in the beyond.

Loving allows seeing the beauty of all things.

Loving is used to develop our capabilities to see the beauty in every human being and in everything. We then realize that they are fine just the way they are and that nothing is ever missing or lacking.

Each individual has a certain beauty that shows through his actions or gestures at one point or another. To focus only on what fascinates or makes us wonder about any individual, or anything, enables our capability to love so much easier, loving it exactly the way it is.

We realize that imperfection is just as pretty as perfection and the individual who commits errors or who is caught red-handed in ego is not any less prettier than the one who is more fulfilled or serene. We see the beauty there is to learn and that every one has his own beauty. This is fantastic in itself and we cannot stop wondering about it, once we see it with the eyes of our heart.

By seeing beauty in everything, each thing becomes lovable in itself and therefore is so easy to love it.

Once we have developed a really intense inclination to love, we cease separating all that exists into what is lovable and what is not. Or, into what is good and what is bad. We reunite all the separated parts of everything to love the whole as it is, because all is lovable within itself without separation or distinction. These mental tricks and superficial adjustments are no longer required for us to love. When we visualize the presence of God in everything, we can also see it in every component of anything. Each part, without exception, becomes lovable and acquires its good side or the quality of being loved for what it is. We sometimes have to look far behind, but the divine presence is always there!... And all there! Why do we refuse to see the divine principle that is in everything? Why do we prevent ourselves from loving it? Why do we deprive ourselves from a greater happiness?

We never tire of loving once we look at all that comes by visualizing the presence of God. We feel the bliss and grace in a sort of continuous contemplation state of trance. Within ourselves, we let our inclination and liking to love predominate and we reassure the rest of what we are. We love all human beings and all things without exception. Whoever we meet is dignified and worthy of love in our eyes. All that happens is beautiful, perfect and complete within itself, even if our human eye could see the opposite in it. With our mind, we stop searching for what could be more beautiful or better, and for what could be missing in any thing or any situation. We stop relying on the impetuousness of our mind to search for things that could make us happy. Instead, we just feel in our heart what is complete on the outside and full in all its aspects. We feel all that exists holds a fulfillment for ourselves. We no longer question ourselves in order to understand why the things and the situations are as they are; we simply accept them with delight and peace.

This is how we can really appreciate all things by visualizing and taking note that nothing is missing. By appreciating it the way it is, we can love it with so much ease. This principle also applies to any human being.

Once all is complete within itself, happiness can no longer escape us!

We feel that we become one with happiness and that we are totally present with all that exists in front of us or far away. We tame happiness to make it an inseparable partner for life.

Thus, we can no longer escape our destiny of becoming beings of love and light. We start being this way, and assuming it on earth, in a union with God which becomes more and more perfect, as we see God and feel it in everything we do. Nothing is missing because it is filled from within and from our heart that changes our vision on all that exists on the outside. This is what's useful about opening our heart to love!... Because a closed up heart could never allow so much happiness; it can hardly make up for what is missing on the outside.

By filling ourselves from within, we trust ourselves so much that we know, without any doubt, that we will always be happy in the future. We realize it and we feel that our happiness becomes "ours" since anything can make us happy. All that exists is only a pretext to make our love and happiness burst out and become visible in the outside world. Happiness merges with us to become us. "WE ARE HAPPINESS" and this is what we feel deep in our heart.

We no longer want violence, hate and "non-love." We choose to love ourselves in all circumstances and under any condition. Nothing can separate us from our heart anymore. Nothing can divide our heart from God or from all that exists. There is only beauty all around us and as far as we can see, because we know in our conscience and our heart how much everything that exists is beautiful. We see it with the eyes of our heart.

We stop judging the good as right or decent and the evil as wrong or bad. To just recognize, a means for learning, a means that allows the apprenticeship for loving more all that exists. In this heavenly universe, we can recreate joy and happiness at all times and as much as we want... We create magic!

Like magic,
we transform all that surrounds us
to make it a pretext for happiness.

What surrounds us is our universe, and the universe I am talking about here, my dear friends, is the ordinary, the daily routine, what we live, the society and the world we live in. Now there is the paradox and the contrast! How can it be like this?... Simply because we can see the good side of everything and the beauty they release. Simply because we adapt quickly to all that exists, instead of trying to change it. We accept and welcome it as it is presented to us. We reconcile with the material world because it is an extension of God, who has already been warmly welcomed in our heart. Every day starts off good, be it rain or storm, it won't change us because the beautiful sun of summer is always in our heart; the sun that produces the face of God... the face of God reflects in our soul and love prevails as king and master. A positive vision of all that happens comes from this and it is then so easy to love life!... to love our life as it is! We see life with contemplating eyes and a compassion that we push to extremes.

Some of you might think I am contradicting myself or that I am confused. But if I'm confused, I can say to them that I am happy! Very happy, and functional in society too! On top of it, my happiness is a pledge of prosperity and success! It is a sure path that will take you there as well.

What is left to look for? Why change? I have integrated myself without really doing it, in a kind of reconciliation with all that exists and all that happens, all simply by loving it and for better loving it to remain in peace. That's how love is useful, to be able to remain in peace and comfortable with myself in all types of situations, and to ease my integration to life as it is lived in our society.

I know that love feeds all that exists and allows it to evolve towards light, so it can hold now and forever more love! If you like, look at us as a head light in a storm. You will arrive safely at the harbor, the harbor of love, where you are all expected and have appointments. I see the road in front of me, a golden road, and I wish you only love!

Seeing with the eyes of the heart is seeing all that exists as beautiful and lovable.

Seeing with the eyes of the heart and soul is allowing happiness at all times. Allowing ourselves to be happy. It is seeing the divine principle and God in all, that eliminates all suffering and all ugliness. If you want to be happy, do it and love until you lose reasoning. Love without trying to understand why and you will be happy! Stop asking yourself why do you love? What importance does it make? Not much in fact! Very little!... I bet you that this happiness that your love will invent will be more intense than anything you can

can obtain or feel on the material or physical plane, or by sexual pleasure, money or any other way you already know!

All that the physical world can suggest does not bring enough happiness. That's the problem!... No lasting happiness... It's as simple as that and this is how I, Gilles, have started to look elsewhere for more satisfaction. I have become more and more spiritual, all by staying practical. Finally, I have detached myself and I have surrendered everything to God. I have let go of my point of references that I used in the past to live my life, and my mind has found itself short of structures, which has allowed me to let go of the stiffness.

To abandon and surrender oneself, we need to have confidence and break the knots that stop harmony and abandonment. We need the certainty that happiness will be at the "rendezvous," even though nothing leads us to predict it.

If not, we continue to worry and we cannot surrender ourselves properly. We won't do it with our whole being, because we will still have a doubt; there will be a certain lack of harmony somewhere and we don't want that. If we don't know exactly how to do it with our whole being, we can still do it as we are and with our disharmonies, so we can continue to learn and improve ourselves. It all depends on if it's what we want. It is a precious awareness to observe our lack of harmony because it triggers the process of dissolving our disharmonies.

Being all in one piece in all we are eases the achievement of happiness. Of course, we need to be on the right track to do so!... On the one where the heart respects the soul's intentions. This way, we can love with all the dimensions of ourselves without leaving any of them aside. It is easier to love this way, because we can form a part of all that exists and make one with it without putting anything aside. Nothing within us is rejected and nothing on the outside can be either. There is reciprocity and consistency and nothing can reduce the intensity of our love.

Surrendering ourselves completely allows us to love better.

If we make many mistakes before we can love this way, it is an obvious sign that we are making progress and going ahead, because we always learn from our mistakes even if this starts with our unconscious mental zone. At least, the information is registered somewhere within ourselves, and, at the right time, it will reach our conscience through our conscious mental zone because of our soul. Then, it will have its effect. On the learning aspect, all of our mistakes and failures are only additional stages that make us advance towards the achievement of a full and satisfactory life where the art of loving will be well tamed or well mastered.

The long, long walk always ends with the nicest victory: the one of learning to love ourselves and learning to love more each stage or each cycle of our life; the one of being happy at all times, by assuming ourselves as we are: beings of light full of love!

Shade can not stop the light in the soul of each of us from coming through. In fact, the shadow is also the beginning of light, a light in its more preliminary form, a becoming light that will be soon visible and recognized by all of us. It's only a question of delay before the change occurs. All is a question of time and evolution for our light to show itself in the physical world. The soul doesn't only hold a potential for light, it is light and nothing can stop its divine intention from triumphing.

Nothing can stop love from being victorious and miraculous!

No spirit in quest for light that clings to our energetic bodies!... nothing!.. all the strength and power in the immature entities of the "astral" can do nothing about it. What is the use of clinging to our bodies?... If not but to learn... to learn about our light... I invite them to cling to me if they wish to, and it's with joy that they will see the light always triumph. I have already demonstrated to a few of them that the light exists and their influence could no longer determine my behaviors and state of being.

It is with compassion and love that I would also like to help them. They deserve our love just like the other more evolved spirits. Now, I love them and I am no longer afraid of them because I know them better. I know they are in the process of becoming beings of love and that they don't know quite yet what love and loving are. If it is what God wants, I am willing to help them right away.

None of the influences coming from non-love can destabilize or divert my behaviors towards shade, hate or fear. I have chosen love. I like love! I like loving! I reconfirm without stopping, my choice to love. I choose to love me as I am and no matter what I am. I don't even wonder how much better I could be; it no longer makes a difference. Being perfect no longer bothers me, because I have let go of these mental concepts and the only thoughts that fascinate me are the ones which strengthen my vibrations of love.

I like to love so much that all is a pretext to love and all leads me to love. I see love everywhere and in everything because my eyes are eyes of love that see further than appearances. I see love in an embryonic state, there, where it could be and where it will be someday. I see love in a secondary state and in a trance. I always see it because I have the intuition of love, a flair to find it even if it is well hidden, because I like love and I have made it mine to share with you.

Love is like a word that we love to pronounce. We are wild about talking love. We feel so much joy doing it. It is so simple and easy to say the truth and to testify what we really do without trying to add on to impress you. Our mind doesn't have to work so hard to make up nice stories or to invent unrealistic ones. Our mind is almost at rest, because it is our heart that is active... and so active!

You could do like me if you want to be happier. Visualizing love is a guarantee of happiness. That is what this visualization is for and that is why we love. All this can be learned, and you can learn too! You can even learn to have love appear where there is none.

Truly loving transposes us in the secondary state.

I love and recognize my soul... I recognize its tiny voice which always penetrates through all that exists and all that can happen to me. I choose love because I choose joy. Now these have become inseparable. The love and joy have become one as a harmonized whole, because my mind has no other function but to reproduce love as it is in my soul on the outside.

My life has not always been as pleasant to live as now. I have felt other feelings which have made me suffer time and time again and which have made me react very immaturely. No thanks, not for me! Finished! I've had enough! I left suffering behind; I'm leaving once again and confirming it! Finished! I choose love because I like love. I like to love and I can repeat it a million times, always with the same joy in my heart and the same peace in my soul: "*I like to love because it brings so much joy and peace!*"

My intentions are praiseworthy: "They are to simply exist the way I am, because this is the way I am happy..." By being myself and assuming all together my human and divine aspects on a daily basis, in the respect of who I am and all that exists... That completes the picture of my driving strength.

Loving is used to build our happiness on solid ground and this includes ourselves, but without restraint to it. If not, our love would return to its mental characteristics. As before, it would be incomplete, limited and restrictive.

By continuing to love and be happy, we come to a position of recreating the conditions that make us live the greatest love, love with a big "L!"

I live the greatest love!

I live "love with a big L." I am in love with someone good... with my man. I need him to be happy and to love. I depend on him to feel love.

I love him as he is and he doesn't need to better himself for me to love him. I love him and will always love him because he suits me perfectly. I love him as I would like him to love me and that's all. I only ask to love him, even if he commits blunders or if he talks nonsense. I am capable of understanding and feeling a grand compassion for him, because me and him, we are one in the same.

No one on earth could ever deviate me from the love I feel for my man. With him, I am safe of all emotional sorrows and I never need to beware or worry about whether he would cheat on me or lie to me tomorrow. I can totally trust him.

I surrender myself to him, for him, with him, within him and with all I can be. I merge with him. I am in love with the man of my life, the ideal man...

My man is myself!

The man I love is me, with all that I am... my personality, my body, my soul, etc...I LOVE MYSELF AS I HAVE ALWAYS WANTED TO BE LOVED BY OTHERS, in fact, as I have always wished to do it... as I am with all that I have been able to be. I have learned to do it and I love myself more than I ever did before. No one else but ourselves can play this role and deserve as much love. We can always count on ourselves to lean on for laughter, crying, sympathy, to pour out all our love from our heart and, on top of it, to feel all our love. All this to find ourselves, to return to our deep essence in order to build our happiness on solid grounds. Because nothing can be more solid than ourselves as a foundation of what we wish to live in our own life. We discover ourselves under a new day, not to become egocentric or filled with ourselves, but to open up more towards ourselves, to better love ourselves and better love. The result is that we turn naturally towards others. This is not a goal within, but a consequence of our grand opening toward ourselves.

Opening toward ourselves is offering ourselves the reconciliation of our human and divine aspects in deep peace and harmony... A beautiful and soft peace that is so relaxing!... An Oasis where we can finally halt to take the time to breath and appreciate our so called, "little happiness." By being peaceful, we discover within ourselves the equivalent in joy and pleasure of all we can find in others, men or women. Once we turn towards others, it is no longer to beg for what we want, but to love them and share with them our joy, all that we have or know... In fact, sharing the "little happiness" that we have created with almost nothing and all by ourselves... on our own!

The more we direct love towards ourselves, with our thoughts that are used to orient us to it, the more we grasp love from our soul and the more happiness gushes out. The more love we feel in our heart, the more this love asks to shine toward others.

Who else than ourselves can replace us in the major role of loving ourselves at all times, in all circumstances and under all conditions? Who else could do it with as much cleverness and relevance? Who else could take care of all we are with as much availability and loyalty? Who is in a better position than ourselves to always love us better and be faithful in a relationship with us? Who else can understand us better and know what we are feeling at all times? Who else but ourselves can live what we live, appreciate at best our own intentions or well understand our objectives?

Who can love us better than ourselves?

No one but ourselves!... No one! No other person is in a position to love us as we can, with as much authenticity, truth and compassion! No one other than ourselves is as worthy and as dignified to benefit from our love!... It is fundamental to direct it towards yourself! Be its base. It will then be easier for you to extend it to all that exists and give it more strength thereafter. No one else can replace us in the life we have to live and in the role of learning to love and always becoming more conscious. This justifies all the love we can grant ourselves.

Turning towards us to love ourselves is pushing back the borders that limit our access to happiness. By orienting ourselves towards others only to build up our happiness, we prevent ourselves from surmounting all the borders of non-love. These borders limit us in our ways of being. They block the other routes that would bring us to a much bigger happiness, a happiness that would offer a wider range of facets and options.

You are the artisan of your own life, and it is you and you only that can create your happiness!

Your man is yourself!
Your woman is yourself!
The rest is only illusion!

CHAPTER III EXERCISES

1. VISUALIZATION ON BEAUTY

- For everything that you see, and for every human being you know, retain from them only what you consider beautiful and what you like.

- Find what pleases you and what you love and let go of all the rest.

- Forget all the rest and act as if it does not exist anymore.

- Visualize that what pleases you increases and becomes more and more beautiful. It overwhelms you and takes all the place.

- Visualize that everything else does not exist any longer. Forget it completely.

- Take the time to fully contemplate what you create, and let yourself thoroughly feel its pleasant side.

- What do you feel now regarding this thing or this person who was the object of your visualization? How do you feel?

- Compare it with the situation before you did this exercise. Which vision brings you more happiness? Which one contains more joy?

- Repeat this exercise as many times as it is necessary. Visualize different persons, things or events each time.

2. PRAYER SEEKING TO CREATE THE CONDITIONS FOR SURRENDERING

Three times a day, during three months, repeat out loud with conviction and devotion:

"God, I put my fate into Your hands. It is as You wish.

My will is joined and subjected to Your will. I surrender to You all what I want. I let You have it; it is up to You to dispose of it as You wish.

Everything that is happening to me is the best that could happen. I accept everything that is happening to me as You wish. I thank You for everything that is happening to me, and it is with joy that I embrace and welcome it. I feel a great peace and I have nothing left to ask; nothing left to change or replace. Nothing needs to be altered any longer and instead of fighting again to obtain what I want and reach my goals, I let You decide whatever concerns my future.

Everything I have and everything that is happening to me is perfect as it is. I accept it the way it is, because it is exactly what I need right now to learn, to learn to love more and better live my life. Everything I have and everything else that I could have loses it's importance, because my happiness comes from my heart and from my soul, and nothing can change or reduce it."

Feel with your heart and soul the energy that this prayer contains, and the emotions it arouses in you. Prepare yourself to witness great changes taking place within you.

Chapter IV

How Do We Learn To Love?

We learn to love by making visible in the physical world the illusions and blocks that prevent us from loving with our soul and heart. Because we can see them clearly, we then become aware of them and we either transform or eliminate them. We transform our ego and our immaturity to love and light. We become used to interiorizing the messages coming from the outside world in order to well identify the aspects and components of ourselves that need to be transformed, to always reflect more love.

We learn to love in all sorts of ways!

The apprenticeship of loving can take all types of forms, so we can acquire more aptitudes and abilities to love. Very often, at our early stage, we feel the need to distort love and make it conditional or then again, experience only one of its facets. It is in what I call mental love. We then see what this gives us. Friendship, for example, is one of the facets of love that we feel, a way of expressing and exteriorizing it. Once our mind is in the game, it often transforms the impulses coming from our soul by separating the humans that are worthy of friendship from the ones who aren't. Instead of developing a friendly link with all that exists, we restrict ourselves to certain people who we use as pretext to the need of exteriorizing our love. Others are often pushed aside.

Because we want to learn a lot, we may even need to experience hating and ascent the entire process that leads to love from far away. As can be seen, our learning to love can be put in various concrete forms. We materialize our blocks and illusions, which allow us to become aware and dissolve them with love and light.

After having completed appropriate experiences, we acquire more aptitudes to love.

By experiencing different facets of love, we can then better realize what loving is, and we acquire more abilities each time. After a while, we will finally learn what to do and how to come to a position of experiencing love in a more complete way, or then again, as it is in our soul.

In other words, we enter into a better position to love in harmony with all dimensions of ourselves. We always have the right note when we play the piano. We always throw strikes when we throw the ball. If we go to a restaurant, it's because that is where we need to be. As can be seen, right and wrong take a different meaning and all is seen within our love frame without judging.

What we are looking at is seen the way it should be and so on... Our gestures and attitudes find themselves their appropriateness facing the actions that must be taken, or facing situations that happen. Learning to love is useful for that and this is why it is used.

When we learn to love, we often feel the need to experience conditional love and evaluate its consequences. Our love is then situated on the human plane, the one of our ego and personality and it constitutes a very human exchange.

We experience "mental" love to realize that it is not the love as it is in our soul. We are confounded and we can feel humility, the humility of learning. We can fully accept our imperfection as a reality that holds as much beauty as perfection; accept our reality of being human that holds imperfections and immaturity in some of our dimensions. We absolutely need them now in order to be able to learn and evolve towards what we are: "Beings of love and light."

Is it easy to love with our mind?

Loving with our mind is one of the stages that consists of learning to love better. Our mind wants to control and transform the love produced by our heart to suit the requirements of our ego and beliefs. It is difficult because we materialize our illusions on love. On the human plane, we make love conditional and divisible, while it is unconditional and indivisible by essence in our soul.

Not loving at all is the beginning! Loving with our mind is continuing a little further; it is separating and differentiating love in its several components or in various kinds of love, based on what we live at certain stages of our evolution. We choose to retain the ones that we judge as needed to make ourselves happy. When love components grow and evolve towards maturity, they will finally all reunify themselves.

At the level of the soul, love reunifies itself the way it was at the beginning, before the mind grasped and transformed it. There is the undivided love that we separate from a mental point of view and reunify thereafter, when we have become aware of it, and our conscience has become wide enough. All of these stages correspond to new phases of enlarging our capacity to love. We only materialize further our potential for loving in order to create our life with the light in our soul.

Once our awareness grows, we come to accept, admit and integrate the spiritual reality, and we then realize that the many things we divided are reunifying themselves. There is less and less separation in our perception of reality and things. We stop being afraid of and feeling threatened by what is unknown to simply welcome it without pushing it aside.

We realize that love is a whole and when it is a whole, it is unconditional as in our soul. This love predominates and we love differently than we did not so long ago. We love, period! We love without conditions! We love in much simpler ways, without barriers or restrictions. We stop separating what can be loved from what can't be, without defining all kinds of love...and without categorizing it. Love becomes, again, real true love without being labeled with this or that. To become secure within its functioning schemes, our mind needs to invent a thousand kinds of love: Platonic love, passionate love, human love, the love of our children, of our spouse, the love of this, the love of that, etc... It is its logic, he separates to understand...

> *"I, Gilles, know a hundred kinds of love, and have experienced a few of them without ever finding satisfaction. I went from one to another while continuing to seek what love was.*
>
> *Today, I have a better idea of what love is, but I still have a lot to learn and it is in the joy of being humble that I continue to learn! What I have discovered astonishes me because I never thought loving was so simple. Once we have accepted it and love it, our soul helps us so much that loving becomes very easy and natural."*

It is not quite the same with hating, which is still more difficult to live with than loving with our mind.

What is hating?... what is the use of it?...

Learning to love can seem difficult depending on how you go about it. Hating is a good example; it is the starting point of learning to love from far behind. Hating is the start of a long process that always ends with more aptitudes to love. We bring back to the surface dark parts of ourselves where harmony has not yet been created. We test our illusions to finally realize all the annoyance we create for ourselves by assuming them in our life. The process always ends in a balance that must be restored and it is always love that fills in this wonderful role.

At the end of each process, we are always more incited to love and we want to hate less and less. We are consciously reluctant to resume hating again, because we start to realize that we were not comfortable at all by doing so.

By means of hating, we come to realize to what extent it is disagreeable to do so. We want and begin to stop hating once we start becoming aware that it brings a lot of annoyances, and that there are other things to do or live that are better for us. Otherwise, we will not be conscious of the reasons why we feel so bad and we will continue hating.

Hating is a scenario of evolution that is hard to live!

All of our human reactions are used for our apprenticeship to love and nothing is ever lost. Even though our mind forgets it sometimes, our soul always remembers it and learns new lessons each time. While living their life, a great number of people experience hate and anger. They don't do it in pure loss and waste. All that they do is useful for something, more awareness for example, and it all has a purpose.

Their life is their own and it is up to them to live it as they please. Everyone is free to learn his own way. We see in this the love manifested by God who loves us enough to always leave us free and who respects us in all that we have chosen to live.

Without being aware of it at the beginning, the people who are full of hate need to realize what they will feel by experiencing this kind of emotion and how they will feel by hating. What does being full of hate bring us?... Are we happy and comfortable with ourselves?

It is much harder to hate than to love because we feel so bad and it's so complicated. We have to mobilize our whole organism in a state of alarm and tension; putting certain parts of ourselves aside. Disharmony installs itself in some kind of interior contradiction. It is tiring and painful to live it and it never stops.

Since the emotions that come with hate bring little satisfaction and disagreeable feelings, it is only a question of time before we realize it. These people will then start to search to experience other things. In the end, they will discover that experiencing love emotions and feelings are much more gratifying, more natural and far more easier.

Feeling love after having felt hate allows us to compare what is more satisfying for us. We never feel hate in vain; this allows us to see clearer and to better assume our potential for love, with a stronger determination and more will-power, because we have learned in our physical body what hating brings and we no longer want it. It hurts too much and we deeply suffer by feeling it. It is also too heavy to carry... Too painful to support. We sustain our interior fights by paying the full price... large quantities of energy come into conflicts and are completely wasted in vain.

By means of hating, we slowly start wanting to love.

This opening can first be seen at the mind's level. Our mind registers that love makes us feel good when our heart is stimulated by others who love us. Love can then become a mental objective which could evolve thereafter.

Hating is a courageous way of learning to love. It is not an avenue filled with roses, far from it! We walk on thorns and it hurts! Every thing discourages us from hating because it is unnatural and it is not agreeable to live. It is difficult to live hate.

The uncomfortable situation can last a long time before it becomes less painful. There are other ways to learn to love that are much more simple. Directly stimulating our liking and inclination to love, for example, is easier to live and more natural. Hating is one of the most difficult ways to learn. Hating is like accepting an illness in our body. Then, we can understand how we feel when we are sick in order to better appreciate health afterwards. It is not all relaxation, is it?

This approach allows us to eliminate a few of our mental beliefs that do not contribute at all to our happiness. It's like doing a huge clean-up. In the end, we can reflect with more power the light of our soul which may be even brighter, because the transformation of our ego is major and we develop a better position to appreciate love.

> *"I, Gilles, have started my apprenticeship with hate, because I didn't know what to do to be happy and it was my ego that directed my life.*

By demonstrating in broad daylight my hate, my anger and all my frustrations, I have realized with my own eyes to what extent it was painful to choose this avenue to better understand what life was and also to better grasp what was hiding behind all the illusions I had materialized.

I have paid a high price for this apprenticeship. I have learned to love the hard way by suffering so much and living hell on earth for many years. I needed to understand what hating could bring and let me tell you, my dear friends, that life made sure it showed me!

That is how I have learned to love. I have realized that nothing could be more painful to live than hate, and I have stopped hardening myself so that I can be more tender. I have sympathized with all I had been. I have congratulated myself for having the courage to go further within myself to tame the energy that was pushing me to hate. Taming it leads us to knowing it better. Then, I have created the ground and space within myself to become more comfortable with this energy, instead of being panicked and afraid once again and unknowing throwing it on others. As a result, it is with love and compassion that we transform it, and then, a certain harmony installs itself!

Now, I prefer being in peace the way I am than to experience hate ever again. In consequence, I accept my little faults as they are without tormenting myself. To the grace of God!

When all the components of myself will be ready to change to reflect more love, then I will accept change! But only in peace and with softness! Not at the price of feeling hate for a certain part of myself. All of me refuses that any hate or anguish should ever seize my physical body again.

Meanwhile, I consider that I am fine the way I am because I feel comfortable with myself, and relaxed in my body. I accept myself without thinking too much or trying to find out if I have to change or not. It is my soul that decides what I should do and no longer my mind.

My soul is sending messages to my conscience and my mind only materializes its guidelines in the visible world by following the path it draws."

When facing ordeals and burdens, a lot of people have a tendency to close their hearts. Some revolt by using an ordeal as a pretext to burst out their hate and non-love that were sleeping and awaiting to rage within them. Once they have enough of it, they choose to live something else. But to start loving again, they need to re-open their hearts.

What goes on before we resume loving?

To resume loving, we need to transform ourselves and accept what happens to us. We need to work on our personality and it is the soul that prepares the person to the change. Once we have realized to what extent it is painful to hate or assume non-loving, our ego reduces and this does not always happen smoothly. This work needs a preliminary time. In the end, the heart is on the verge of opening, and it only lacks the appropriate urges.

This person can draw these stimulations from within if she desires and chooses to do so. To get there, it is necessary to enlarge our awareness and have a good knowledge of ourselves, which means knowing how we will react to any kinds of varied circumstances. With practice, we learn to permute further our emotions, in order to open our heart and keep it open when circumstances incite us to do the contrary.

What often happens is to wait for others to be stimulated to love. Then, we award them the responsibility of the love we feel. The others who unconditionally love us thus represent a triggering element, an outside pretext or an outlet to our love which is only waiting to wake up.

When someone is on the verge of feeling love, it is because he has prepared himself and his heart has already done the work to be able to open-up at the slightest incitement.

The love of others makes him become aware and reminds him once again that love exists, because we often forget it and we will easily close our heart when facing ordeals and burdens. We need others to remind us because we have a hard time reminding ourselves on our own. We often need ordeals and burdens to learn to remind ourselves, and this is the only reason why we have attracted them in our life.

Since love produces good and agreeable feelings, the person realizes it and is then very incited to feel it himself. This choice can be unconscious. Feeling love is more than realizing it exists with our mind or with our conscience. It's also integrating it and this is what we need to be more happy or retrieve happiness once we have stopped loving.

Everything we go through is useful to learn to love.

If we look further, we notice that people who stop loving or are filled with hate are learning only to love like many others who have chosen different ways to go about it. They want to go to the end of their illusions and they need to surpass them. The more they linger on surpassing them, the more they will be confronted with suffering... And the more suffering grows, the more they will be urged to resume loving and transform themselves.

We see here the way they have learned to widen their conscience, a way that needs great courage and will put them in a position to reflect love with more ability and intensity in their future behaviors. There are other ways to reach the same goal, but it is not up to us to judge why they have chosen this way.

Why do we judge the apprenticeship?

Simply because our liking and inclination to love still needs to intensify so we can love more all that happens. Judging is like fixing and deciding that a reality is finished, whereas nothing is really ever finished in life!

By limiting and imprisoning all that happens within a context of laws and human considerations, we inevitably close-up on the judgment as a way of interpreting life. We look at all that exists with the eyes who want to separate every thing. We decide between the ones who are from our culture or who stick to our beliefs, and others. We separate the guilty from the not guilty, the good from the bad and so on. Our partial and mental vision stops time in the present moment and all that happens is considered as finished. We create artificial barriers with all that surrounds us. These barriers would not exist if we would put ourselves in God's position or if we would look at life from our soul's point of view. Our vision is really only a demonstration and disclosure of our inner divisions and hidden disharmonies to the visible world.

Why stop the apprenticeship on a reality of a moment without seeing and knowing what is next? For sure, something will follow! Then, what's the use of judging now the experimentation of non-loving or hate as bad and finished? Is it to make us aware that our vision of reality and life is incomplete?... It has stopped and stiffened. Stiffening it this way prevents us from seeing other facets of reality and life.

Our vision of things can be enlarged. We see in the process of judgment a mental and simplistic vision of what happens and what exists. This vision denotes that the liking and inclination to love can be intensified, so that the individual who sees things this way can acquire a larger and non-finished vision of what life and evolution are... In summation, a more objective vision of what they really are. Thus, he can acquire a more global and realistic vision of his own life, instead of limiting himself to a vision produced only by his mind that imprisons evolution in the present time. He forgets the future.

> *"I have lived this situation, where my mind urged me to judge others and put them in boxes according to different categories which I thought were appropriate. That reflected the evolution of my conscience at that time.*
>
> *As the years went by, reality showed me at what extent some of my beliefs were limited and non-justified, which allowed me to enlarge my vision of things to take into account the evolution process. I have learned to feel secure without needing to categorize others as if their whole life was decided and finished or as if their whole being was fixed and stiff and has stopped evolving."*

Judging prevents us from attaining a larger awareness of ourselves.

By judging, we veil the door that gives us access to a larger knowledge of ourselves and a more complete vision of reality. We forget why we are here and we make diversions. We lose ourselves in appearances and false evasions and we miss the essential.

We are not on earth to judge how the apprenticeships are done and the way others learn to love. We are here to learn to love, nothing else! We can inspire from others to become more aware of ourselves, if we do not understand how we can learn to love by ourselves on our own. We can also help others if they wish to, by making them understand additional aspects and consequences of different avenues they choose. We can explain why it is this way and where all this will lead them, but the result is not ours because each human is responsible and is the master of his own destiny.

One way or another, humans always assume the consequences of what they chose to live. The balance, the relevance, and the appropriateness between different states or situations that follow each other are always maintained and they match with what we have formerly created. Whether we assume it now or later, what does it change? All will be taken care of and it comes down to the same thing at the end, because for the soul, time does not exist!

By looking at the apprenticeships that are done within the context of this more vast perspective, we realize that our value judgments are futile and, in fact, mean very little. They are subjective and changeable. And if we disregard time, we come to abandon our judgments. If we look at the beginning or at the end of what is done, I mean right after the balance has been re-established, we come up with conclusions or opinions that are diametrically opposed. We realize that our judgments have no longer any foundation and we search within ourselves for the answers of what pushed us to judge. Why do we doubt the universal justice?... The universal laws?... Why do we question the presence, the manifestation or the acceptance from God of all that happens on the human plane? Because that is really the case!

If this was not the case, we wouldn't close-up on judgments and beliefs to feel secure and smother our doubts, but we would seek to see further and know more!

Above the human laws, there are the universal laws.

We can see that universal principles govern all that happens on earth and these give us a more complete and subtle explanation than human laws.

Of course, human laws have their reasons for existing, because they establish beacons and rules for desirable behaviors in society and we can use them as a starting point to facilitate our comprehension of what happens. Starting point means that something else should be added to it to have the whole picture.

What we are saying is that the human being who increases his awareness will be able to realize the existence of grand universal principles that are linked to each human law. And instead of using human laws as a base to judge all that happens and conclude his questioning, he will be able to lean on the universal laws to attain a more vast and complete comprehension of reality. He will then stop judging to go further, rather than smothering his doubts in secure beliefs and opinions from a mental point of view.

One thing is for sure, the universal laws give us a larger and clearer vision of what life and evolution are, while making easier our apprenticeship of loving. We know better what we are aiming for and what will happen in our future. This clearer vision helps us to determine with more precision what we need to learn to be in a position to love better all that exists and to live more serenely and in peace with all that happens to us.

Realizing the existence of the universal laws leads to an energy transfer from our mind to our heart.

The starting point to understand what governs the universal laws[2] is our heart and soul. We feel less of a need to have answers right now to all that happens, to simply accept it in the peace of our soul and with the confirmed intuition and the certainty of what will happen next. Since we go back to the causes of what happens, we know and recognize that they always have their effects. We stop doubting it because we notice that we were able to realize it many times while living our lives. We have a good idea about what the future holds.

Our mind stops bombarding us with questions and it is as if a peace treaty was just concluded with all our dimensions and our heart which becomes, with unanimity, our new headquarters. And our physical body reflects this intense well-being. Our body talks by itself and demonstrates that we are able to live in harmony.

> *"Recognizing the presence of grand and obvious universal laws allowed me to accept loosing certain beautiful dreams I had caressed on the human plane. In return, I realized all I could gain on the spiritual plane by leaving behind what I desperately wanted, not so long ago. This bigger understanding of reality was like the balm on the wounds of my heart, which enabled them to close and heal.*

[2] See Appendix A for the featuring of what is a universal law.

When an individual directs his life from his heart, his mind then stops being like a life-buoy and his vision of things is no longer like a restless sea. He can then drift without fear on calm waters with an inclination to love that lights up his life with happiness."

Seeing with the eyes of the soul is seeing farther than the judgment.

By looking at what happens with the eyes of the heart and soul, we enlarge our vision of things and therefore stop judging the apprenticeship. We see with eyes of compassion and mercy to finally discover that nothing is ever finished.

We discover that "loving" is the goal that each human is seeking and that it is only a question of time before he can reach it. Loving fills him with joy! Nothing can feel as good as the love of our soul! It is why he always aims for this goal, even if he sometimes seems lost or not aware of it. Experiencing the love of our soul in a visible manner brings positive outcomes and we attract, without necessarily needing or wanting it, love and joy that others recognize through us and testify in their neighborhood in reaction to what we have become.

We are in an interrelationship with all that exists, whether we like it or not. The artificial separations we create with our ego, the types of division we invent with our mind and the closure towards others changes nothing, rather they also constitute a choice of relationships. They represent a barometer of the states of our soul and they indicate at what stage of evolution we are in. They also constitute a sure track that can take us within ourselves on the path of a grander harmony. Maybe we need to do a serious clean-up?... To be aware of this, it is up to each of us to be sufficiently honest towards himself.

It is up to each of us to determine what is convenient to experience depending on our own needs of apprenticeship. We do not support or approve hate as a way to learn to love, no more than any other way either. The question we need to ask ourselves is this one: Do our choices respect the will of our soul and do they contribute to easing the achievement of our plan of life? We need to look at what happens in a perspective of evolution. In this sense, every way can be good depending on what we need to experience and to learn to be able to draw out more love from our soul.

On the other hand, we must be ready to accept living with the consequences of our choices. If we throw rocks at others to learn to love, it is very possible that those rocks will be thrown back at us, *because we create the conditions for its occurrence.* We then see where all of this is leading us, and by seeing with our own eyes what it is, we can start to change. This is how balance is re-established.

Once we have benefited from the lessons of all we had to live in learning to love, we are incited more and more to love. It becomes easier and easier. We are also less and less incited to hate as we continue to live our life. We only wish to experience love. It is the ultimate stage.

What most people find difficult is not to convince themselves that they want to learn to love, but to "KNOW WHAT TO DO" to get there. A lot of famous words tell us that the goal to attain is loving with intensity, but often we don't know what to do and carry out in order to achieve it. For example, how do we start from where we stand to reach such results? The large majority of human beings ask themselves this question.

"Love the others as yourself."

Now here are beautiful and famous words in which every one subscribes to. The problem that most people run into is not related to the acceptance of what this message contains, but knowing how to assimilate, assume and integrate it into their daily lives. How to implement it?

First of all, what is the meaning of these love words? What is their deep meaning? We understand what we want from love, depending on where our conscience is in its evolution. We then give love different definitions.

We can believe in love with our mind, making it a mental objective that we desire to reach. We see it clearly and concretely when certain people say they love themselves, yet they are not in peace and are not happy. Because, if they would truly love themselves with their heart and all their dimensions, they would be happy and in peace.

Others feel love in their hearts by being inspired by the outside world to be able to do so, and this is because of their beliefs that limits them to this scenario and therefore limits their love. The outside plays an essential role that allows them to love and stimulate it. Some also draw love from their soul without always being able to continuously reflect it in the visible world, while others, more experienced, are able to do so on their own and with more frequency.

Anything we say reflects the progress we have made in our apprenticeship to love.

In the questions that some people ask, we can notice what stage they have attained in their spiritual evolution, this progress being in fact, a long walk in the apprenticeship of the art of loving. For example, what do we do to love our neighbor if we don't love ourselves enough? Or then again, how do we love ourselves in order to love our neighbor?

These are not the deep motivations of the human being, but only mental manifestations of his true motivations that his rational and logical mind has recovered. These questions on love are of a mental nature. It looks like there are many kinds of love and that is not what is lived in the soul, because at this particular level, love is a unified whole. Furthermore, these questions come from mental considerations and separations that are privileged by the mind which brings love back to logical and rational objectives on different but very human planes.

The real question and the problem that many individuals encounter is what to do to have or increase their liking and inclination to love, and in consequence, be able to love?... And to be able to feel love?... How do we increase our capability to feel love as it is in our soul?...

The words that I have quoted above clearly define that the love of ourselves and the love of others is a whole that is reconciled and reconcilable at all times. It also indicates that it is the way of loving that its author recommends.

If you don't love yourself, you can not love others. We can attempt to adopt behaviors that seem like those of love, but sooner or later, our lack of harmony, resulting from non-love, will resurface. And if you love yourself a lot, you are in a position to also love others a lot, because love is a whole indivisible and this is done simply and naturally.

For many people, the sweet words of famous preachers contribute in increasing their questioning about love or to increase their inclination and liking to love... So, to increase the love they could feel for all that exists? A fundamental question still permeates their mind: What do we do to love?... How do we love?... I would like so much to love further, but I do not know yet what to change in myself to achieve it.

The increases of our inclination and liking to love stimulate our desire to learn to love.

By talking about love with others, we often feel that our liking and inclination to love increases because our heart is made to love and is stimulated. It is easy to stimulate it to love since the individual feels good in such a case and gets a sense of well-being by doing so, but our mind might continue resisting. Even if our liking and inclination to love is stimulated, we still don't know how to be in order to feel love and to love on a continuous basis... Especially, how to reflect it in our daily activities. Our liking and inclination to love are still not intense enough to reach all the different aspects and dimensions of ourselves and to create harmony between them. What can we do to achieve this? How can we create this harmony and materialize our inclination to love on a solid basis in actions?

It is when we ask ourselves such questions that our desire to learn to love grows, because we already have the liking and inclination to love. At the beginning, this has an impact on our mind which makes it an objective: "*Who can show it to me? Learning to love excites me! What is loving with my soul? What is love? What do we feel and how are we when we love? What do we do to feel it?*"

All of this is unknown! To be able to love all that surrounds us properly, we need to draw love from our soul, and with our conscience that should have necessarily enlarged itself, we also need to be able to realize how we act. Once it is sufficiently enlarged, loving with our soul is no longer unknown and we become able to love all that exists.

This becomes very familiar. By using our conscience in the appropriate way and with wisdom, we can remove obstacles and anything that could prevent us from loving with our soul. We can choose it, because we clearly know what we do when we love with our soul. And since the first time, we have become aware of it, we always can remember, because of our enlarged conscience that helps us without failing. It is harder to love with our soul without using our conscience, because we don't know what we are really doing that way. If we don't understand what happens to us at this particular moment when we feel it, how can we really choose it thereafter?

By certain reactions of our physical body, we realize in concrete terms what are the manifestations of our soul and we can become aware of it that way. We realize what occurs within ourselves when we enter deep at our soul level. Without anything inciting us, we suddenly feel very intense bursts of emotion in our chest. It all becomes clear and we always understand better the reality of the moment and what we should do.

When we feel love as it is in our soul and we realize what this love is with our conscience, then the ways of being and doing things that would allow us to reflect it in the physical world automatically graft themselves to what we feel. We no longer think about what we have to do to love with our soul. Now, no questions subsist at our mind's level. No more resistances to love! The questions of the mind, that wanted to understand, recover and grasp love to make it an objective, make sense no longer in our eyes. It is all linked to itself in the logic of love and our mind has no other choice, but to rally to our conscience who has a more vast comprehension of what is going on.

Our mind is surpassed by the motivations of our soul that indicates to us the route to follow to love and reflect our love in all that we do. Our mind becomes as an instrument to only serve our soul and to help it to reflect in our actions what we feel. It appears and acts only at this stage to transform our ways of being in ways of acting in love or out of love. Our ways of being are determined by the love we feel in our heart and is taken from our soul. Our mind no longer determines the objectives by itself due to an outside stimulus, because it is annexed to our conscience that is nourished from our soul.

The following text constitutes a modern way of updating our objective to love in the energy context of today.

Love with your soul and your love will become like the radiant sun!

"Love all that exists, as your soul is capable of doing it!... The way it knows how! Merge your personality and your ego with your soul to reflect in broad daylight all the light it holds and you will see how easy it is to love all that exists without distinction... Yourself or others, it is the same thing! You will only see fire... the fire that will come from your ecstatic feeling. Your love will radiate like a marvelous sun for all that surrounds you, and also for yourself at the same time! Your love will shine the light of your conscience. There will be the merging of

your love with all that exists: things, human beings, God, etc... All that exists is united and interrelated; any part has its reasons to exist and to be loved without distinction and that's why it was created.

Why do you separate all that is united and lovable in itself? Why separate?... To love only certain parts of it?... The ones you select on purely artificial grounds and that your mind privileges! Why do you put aside the rest which is just as lovable as what you have retained for your aims to love? That is not your souls' point of view! Your soul wants you to assume your potential for loving and to realize that all can be loved without condition.

Your soul wishes that you use its light to develop your potential for love, and this with the precise goal that you can live your life in joy. This is why and only why you have this potential! And that is why it is waiting to be discovered by your heart!"

It is much easier to live our life in joy when all that exists can be loved simply for what it is. We can achieve this by transforming our heart to be able to keep it always open, wide open.

Once we feel well-disposed to love all that exists the way it is, similarity, relevance and reciprocity then install themselves between what we have become and all that exists. The link is harmonized and there is a merging, an energy exchange and a synergy in cooperation and complementary with ourselves. Our place in the Universe is perfectly well defined towards all that exists, and all that exists returns itself by making us understand that we have taken our place. All this is seen with the eyes of our soul and by placing ourselves at this level to see it from this point of view.

How do we love with our soul?

Loving with our soul is to make use of all the components, the aspects and the dimensions of ourselves to love with harmony. Like joyful accomplices, all our components work together to achieve this goal.

It is also drawing love from our soul to make sure that the love, as it is at this level, becomes visible in the outside world, without any changes. This love that is shown to all is unconditional. Once we express unconditional love, we often do it from our soul. THEN, LET'S STOP SAYING WE CAN'T LOVE WITH OUR SOUL because WE DO IT OFTEN without even realizing it! It is not because we aren't aware of it that we don't do it. Let's stop making mysteries with simple demonstrations of the impulses from our inner self!

Loving with our soul is making sure that our love can transcend[3] all our ways of being and all our feelings that are on the plane of our personality and ego. Not to be transformed or blocked at this level, because it will lose its purity or its essence.

The love, as it is in our soul, is also seen without change in our actions. We just testify it. It is always free of any condition and brings happiness each time we live and assume it on earth. Once we have increased our awareness and enlarged our conscience, we can recognize this love and marvel at it. To love this way, our personality must accept allowing our soul to transcend it. We can learn to do this more and more often, because everyone does it at one time or another. Then, again, LET'S STOP SAYING WE CAN'T DO IT!

---

[3] The same author has written a book in French on this topic (How to transcend our ego to feel more love). This book presents the key principles that could allow you to do it successfully.

Loving with our soul while living our human life implies that all our chakras and all our bodies can give way to the demonstrations of our soul without blocking them. The personality and ego must embrace collaboration with the soul in a harmony that prepares their fusion.

To be able to love with our soul, we need to make adjustments at the level of our bodies and chakras.

Before all the conditions are met to be able to love with our soul, our channel, which is formed with our seven major chakras, must be opened and liberated from the blocks and restrictions that prevent the energy of love from passing through freely on a continuous basis. The opening is maintained by our chakras, no matter what we are confronted with. This often requires having experienced ego in each of them to learn our lessons before we become able to do it in any circumstance.

Our bodies must become more subtle for the same reason, because if their ego's area is too large, they will not allow vibrations high enough as the one coming from our soul. Increasing our intensity and our vibration frequencies ease a lot the passage of the energy from our soul. If not, even if our channel is open, there will often be disharmonies and interference because of the ego in our bodies. The love, as it is in our soul, will have difficulty to reach the physical world and to be visible by the eyes of everyone. Certain programming of our invisible bodies can form blocks to the demonstration of our love at its purest state.

To be able to exteriorize the love from our soul, we should also listen to what our physical body has to say in order to avoid disharmonies at this level. We have to maintain a certain state of well being and the physical conditions that are required to sustain high vibrations in our other bodies. Never forget that it is in our entire physical body that we live our life. By creating physical disharmonies, we cannot reach deep and lasting happiness, because these disharmonies will manifest themselves in our life to make sure we will transform them.

Loving with our soul allows us to love all that exists as it is, including all the aspects of ourselves, our qualities and our faults. This also includes the qualities and the faults of others and all this is put on the same level to be loved without distinction.

Once the light of our soul reaches our conscience, we are then able to neutralize all interferences that could prevent our love from radiating like the majestic sun. The light of our soul reflects far beyond our conscience and comes to enlighten all who seek happiness and who want to love. Our light only asks to shine for each and everyone of us without distinction. We are all friends and members of the same family.

Like any other ability, we can learn and acquire the ability to love with our soul.

Once the required adjustments are done at the level of our bodies and chakras, it becomes relatively easy to love with our heart and soul. It is even a little simplistic and it has nothing mysterious. This becomes very concrete, when the love we originally feel in our heart is spread among all the cells of our physical body, to reflect all together the state of harmony we have reached. Loving this way is so relaxing. We have nothing to do; to only be in contact with all we see and all we feel that is invisible; to welcome it with our physical body, as it is or as it is presented to us; to only feel what is released from all that exists to love it as it is; to vibrate and form a part of all we see in order to let everything or everyone know how we feel for them, and that we love them for what they are. Within ourselves, we converse and have dialogue with them in some sort of simplistic loving relationship. We imagine the answer and feel it in our heart. We generalize this effect to our entire physical body. There's always more love to feel and it's easy to do. We feel so good by loving and by welcoming all that exists... And we do it in an almost innocent way.

We place ourselves at the level of our soul when we orient our conscience and our thoughts to act as if we WERE only our soul in all we live. We imagine that our whole being has become only our soul, and we try to compare with what we usually are to highlight the differences in our attitudes and behaviors. We rely on our soul to love and we practice to make sure that our soul transcends our personality for the purpose that it radiates in the physical world. As we often visualize this transcendent, we end up doing so with more and more ease, somewhat like an automatic reflex.

Praying and meditating are good ways that predispose us to put ourselves at the level of our soul to live our daily lives. If you don't know what to do to feel the presence of your soul, why not start here and practice! It's only a question of time before you obtain good results.

Joy, voluptuousness, bliss, ecstasy, and grace are signs that indicate at what extent we master the art of loving with our soul. If we cannot feel any of the above sensations, this means that we still have room to learn further to love, in order to be able to do so.

Once we master more the art of loving, we learn to reflect love on the outside, the way it is in our soul. Letting love burst out as it is in our soul is loving all that exists without exceptions, and without conditions. This is done simply and humbly, without thinking to do it. It is living continuous happiness and paradise on earth, or elsewhere when we are deceased. Because nothing can change our feelings!

Being in a physical body or not doesn't change much when we strongly feel this love, because we unite with God to form a new entity together with him. We surrender ourselves totally to God, with all our bodies and chakras and invent for us a new identity. There is no more room for separation, because we are unified with all that exists and we have re-joined and put all together all our dimensions and components within ourselves. No more missing pieces in the puzzle! Our components have re-united all together and are linked within themselves by love. They are gathered together in a homogeneous whole to recreate a harmonized and synergetic ensemble. There is a certain harmony within ourselves which allows us to be able to keep our heart open at all times.

Loving with our soul brings bliss and wonder.

The more we feel love, the more we can marvel at all that exists. We marvel at the greatness there is in everything and at the beauty that is always present. We develop a state of grace and we feel immense joy.

Do you think that the capability of being marveled with the most boring things removes our energy of action? Not at all! It is the contrary, we become stronger!... Stronger in everything we do or we get used to doing. We are still capable of acting in society... We are real "doers!"... Well integrated

Because increasing our capability to be marveled with anything so trivial, gives us strength at all levels. We can live our material lives and assume ourselves at the physical level with even more skills than before. It all depends on what we want or if it is what we need to be happier.

"My own example demonstrates it because the others see me as a practical and efficient businessman and I feel the presence of God in all I do and in all that happens to me. Seeing God in the material things is a challenge I created for myself to better love my work. Being in a position to love more my employees, my associates and my clients allows me to understand them more completely, to serve them better, and to better adapt my services to suit their real needs. It is with eyes of compassion that I serve them. It is with joy that I live my life. Working in these conditions is much more enjoyable than before and it is I who have chosen to be this way.

You can do like me if you want, because I am no more smarter than you! I am like you! I do not meditate perfectly and I accept to be disturbed when I seek to collect myself to pray. Keeping good contact with all that surrounds me, a friendly contact full of kindness is more important to me than meditating or praying well, which is not an end in itself. When I stay peaceful while nothing incites me to do so, it is what I call achieving my goal, transcending my ego and relying on my soul to integrate peace in my daily routine that meditation could otherwise bring me. All is perfect this way and I learn to put up with the unexpected that presents itself to simply welcome and love it."

At one point in time,
we all feel love as it is in our soul.

We all have a soul that allows us to feel unconditional love. We all feel unconditional love sooner or later. Who has never loved his spouse, a child, or a parent without wishing him happiness at all times and at any price? What type of love is this? Think about it for a few minutes!... These are not the characteristics of conditional love, but of unconditional love that comes from the heart and soul. To love this way, you transcend your personality and you place yourself at your soul's level, without even noticing or being aware of it. You could do it more and more often if you wanted to!

What we need to do is learn to generalize and extend this love to more people and more circumstances. This happens with experience and experimentation. But we need to want it, to choose and practice it, so we can feel more and more the presence of our soul within ourselves.

DARKNESS IS NOT REALLY DARKNESS!

In all darkness,
 there is always a glimmer of light
 that is waiting to manifest itself.
I visualize it
 with the eyes of the heart
 and I imagine it with the eyes of love.

Darkness
 is only a becoming light!
All that is missing,
 is the starting sparks to light it up

for it to disperse itself,
so we can see a bit clearer.

Each of us
represents this enlightenment.
I am this spark
and I cease to identify
darkness to darkness and
shade to shade
because I know that my light
has already left
a ray of clarity,
a glimpse of hope.

There is no shadow organization,
but it is I who create its strength
by my fears and my inner divisions,
my separation between shade and light.
This is how
we maintain it in place
and strengthen it,
and by this way,
we do not contribute
to the spreading of light.

Let's stop giving tags
to all that is existing

to see further...
see evolution and light
that are coming.
There is only immaturity
and unconsciousness...
Light in horizon on different planes.

At the limit,
there is only God who is love.
There is only our own shadow
that can attract its counterpart,
its taking part on the outside.
There is only us facing ourselves
with the only choice
to love shade or to be afraid of it.

...Because shade can become light,
only under the impulsions of love
and not from judgments and battles.

Since my inner battles are over,
I don't need any weapons
to fight against shade,
But simply to love it
with compassion and mercy.

My love will know
how to perform the miracle
of bringing a little clarity
where the need is pressing.

My love will demonstrate
to what extent it is good to love.
It will make others aware,
others that don't know,
that love exists deep within themselves too!

All I have is full confidence
in the power of my love,
and that's it!
Nothing else is necessary!

Since I enjoy spreading light,
I have learned to love shade,
and I love it now.
I am no longer afraid of it,
because I have tamed my own fear.

Loving shade
is the most efficient and fastest way
to transform it into light.

Because nothing can resist to love
  and nothing can resist
  to my inclination to love.
Everything is a pretext for me to love,
  and shade is the nicest of pretexts.

There is no place of darkness on earth;
  there is no place
  where shade predominates or triumphs;
  there are only places
  where love is missing
  and where learning is done.

Since I look at all that happens
  with love,
It's only a question of time
  before light will appear and burst out.

I feel, deep in my gut,
  that evil is to learn the good,
  and hatred, to learn the love,
  and I see with my own eyes
  that I am triggering big changes...
Miracles could even occur soon, that
way...
  because pure love is miraculous...
  and the heart of the one who hates

or does bad
is only asking to open to this love,
to love again and be happy.

I invite all
who or what we can classify as dark
or the strength of shade
to cling onto me.
I have no protection
and I don't need any.
Humans do not need wars,
as they need love,
and I am confident
that the divinity of each individual
will know how to triumph
under the impulse of love.

I offer
and surrender myself to God,
with the peacefulness of my soul,
with the love of my heart,
and in full trust.
In his arms,
what could happen to me?...
Nothing other
than the best that could happen.

Love does not make war.
Love does not need shields
  or swords.
Love is a strength
  that is present in all that exists,
  and our love only reconciles
  the link that joins us to it.

Shade is no exception.

Our happiness becomes immense
  and it seals this harmony
  at the heart's level
  where the soul transcends
  and merges to it.

CHAPTER IV EXERCISES

1. GUIDELINES TO IDENTIFY THE APPRENTICESHIPS THAT YOU NEED TO MASTER FOR LOVING MORE

- Begin by identifying and selecting the important events of your life that have left you with a strong imprint.

- Choose an event and describe briefly, on a piece of paper, what you have experienced and lived.

- On another sheet of paper, indicate what would have happened if you would have lived the same event, but with more love? What would have happened, if you would have felt more love in your heart? What would you have done? How would you have been?

- Compare the results of each sheet in order to identify the apprenticeships that are left to integrate and master.

- Establish a tie between the way you have lived this event and your apprenticeship to love. Make out the links. In what way has this experience contributed to help you to learn further to love? What did you learn from this event and what is left to learn for you to love better and more deeply? See the direct or indirect ties... because there are always some when we look through the eyes of the soul. For example, to get to the bottom of one's illusions is an indirect way to prepare the ground to improve your loving capabilities in similar circumstances. And in the future, you will notice the difference, because you will be able to live a similar event, but this time, feeling more love and serenity.

- Point out thoroughly the apprenticeships that are being made. Identify them clearly. These apprenticeships resemble a bridge between what you have been, and what you believe you could have been. You can identify them by finding out what would have enabled you to be what you have just mentioned in the case you would have felt more love. These learning opportunities are like the missing link, and it will become easier to make the equation the more you look at them.

- Focus your attention inside of you and assess your situation. Where do you stand in your apprenticeship to love? What would you do if a similar event were to come up unexpectedly in your life right now?

2. GUIDELINES TO INCREASE YOUR KNOWLEDGE ON UNIVERSAL LAWS

- Verify, if during that same event, your vision about life or any other thing was limited by judgments.

- If it was the case, indicate the limits of your love that your judgments would have created. Identify the principles, the reasoning and the rationale that prevented you to manifest further your love.

- Look beyond what you see! What would have happened if you would have let your heart and your soul express themselves more, instead of your mind and your personality?

- Under such circumstances, let your heart take a much greater importance and lead you to its peaceful ways of being. Then, identify the universal laws and principles that will allow you to go beyond the judgments.

- In order to do that, place yourself at the level of your soul and make out the links with the experience you have lived. What would have happened if you would have been more loving?

- Allow your soul to vibrate, and identify which basic quality (kindness, respect, integrity, compassion, trust, generosity, mercy, love, etc...) could have changed significantly the outcome of the event that took place.

- What would have followed if this quality would have been manifested? You will then be able to define the cause and the effect as well as the universal principles that are tied to the judgments you have shown. Ask your spirit guides to help you if you have difficulty in doing this.

- Once you have finished doing these two exercises, start over again using another event until you will have reviewed all the major events of your life.

3. VISUALIZATION TO TRANSCEND YOUR PERSONALITY USING YOUR SOUL

- Ask your soul to focus and to concentrate its energy in your heart.

- Imagine this energy as a powerful electric current, ready to be spread throughout your entire physical body.

- Feel these pushes of energy, starting and pouring from your heart, and imagine them filling all the cells in your body, to invigorate and enlighten them.

- Visualize a movement coming from within you and going outward, and now, see the light it creates.

- Imagine yourself as a gigantic light, sparkling and shining from this electric current.

- Affirm that nothing can prevent your heart and your soul from projecting these rays of light through your entire body, and letting them be seen on the outside.

- Now, from your seven major chakras, visualize seven bright lights:

* red for the base
* orange for the hara
* yellow for the solar plexus
* green for the heart
* light blue for the throat
* dark blue for the third eye
* violet for the crown

- Once again, visualize yourself as this powerful light, like a lighthouse from which everyone can see its beam of light from far away as it was so strong and so bright.

- Now, act as if your entire being was only your soul, and affirm that your soul glows and radiates from all its light, and it has transcended your ego and your personality.

- Feel the vibrations emanating from your soul. With your conscience, realize how you feel. Acknowledge that all your pleasant sensations are, in fact, the manifestations of the unconditional love that your soul produces.

- Thank your personality and your soul for their cooperation, and in your daily activities, while living your life, remember these sensations of joy and the unconditional love that you have drawn by yourself from your soul. Remember the bright light that you have imagined shining from your soul. You can visualize it once again and every time your ego becomes agitated and overbearing.

- Welcome the peace coming from within your soul; it is like a gentle wave quieting the emotional uproar that is about to stir.

Chapter V

SERVING!...
A CONSEQUENCE OF LOVING?

What Is Serving?

Serving is opening more to ourselves by allowing others to benefit from what we are. It is also a consequence of loving, an evident extension of our love, the outcome of what we have become, and a spring board that allows us to be more ourselves.

Serving is a way to materialize even more the presence of our soul in our daily activities. Another way to further demonstrate what we have become. With service, the general public can get to know our soul better; we make it even more visible in everyone's eyes and officialize its demonstrations. Each individual is now able to see what our soul incites us to do and to realize he also has one.

The true benefits that others get from our service are only a consequence of what we have become. Giving and receiving merge together in a kind of bliss that surpasses all the pleasures the material world can offer. Even before we begin to serve, the cycle of energy: "asking, welcoming" is completed and there is nothing left to the circuit... Nothing to ask, nothing to welcome.

Serving is a little like being served.

We feel a vivacious pleasure by serving, a pleasure that we allow ourselves to feel, as a gift we would have offered to ourselves. In fact, we serve in joy and we gather more joy by doing so. Joy is served to us as on a silver platter and we always open the door to more happiness.

Since we are filled with joy and we already feel fulfilled simply by serving, we expect nothing from others, nothing from God or from the beyond. We love all that exists of visible and invisible without expecting or asking anything in return. In fact, there is nothing left to ask for. We only abandon ourselves to God's will. We only feel joy by serving all who are searching for the light or who want to better live their lives, to live it in joy.

We love God. We act with and for him, and we do so with love. We drink at the fountain of universal love that comes from God whom we feel in our hearts. We are satisfied as we are and we need nothing more. So, if you want to be fulfilled, learn to serve, because it is when we have learned to detach ourselves enough to want nothing else, that we attract everything, all that we would have otherwise wanted. The lessons have been learned, and the barriers that were stopping us from being fulfilled are now removed, because we already feel fulfilled. This is how universal law works. What could we want more in the physical world? We feel that we need nothing more than what we have, because we have detached ourselves from everything and we love all that exists. We are more than content with it because we are delighted. We are extremely pleased with everything we already have.

When are we ready to serve?

We are ready to serve when we no longer expect anything from others. We no longer feel the need to dream of what more we could have to be happy. As we expect nothing from others, we are satisfied with all that we have and we only appreciate it for what it is. All that we own has earned the essence of being perfect the way it is.

We have learned to love it only for what it is and not for what it was or could be! Since we are no longer mobilized by all kinds of thoughts at the material level, we become available for ourselves and others. We are available for service without any barriers and we give ourselves total freedom of choosing between serving or not. This makes it easy to serve because we choose it naturally, and because our love has become so powerful that it is only asking to shine and radiate.

The true power of love makes all its sense in the radiance it wants and asks for within itself, and by the only fact it was created. Service is only a channel that receives our energy because it plentifully overflows from us. It allows the power of our love to reach its goal and materialize itself. If not, the energy flow would not be quite completed and fulfillment could not be reached that way.

We cannot be powerful just for ourselves. We can't stop the heart from overflowing of love once it is too full. We can't stop the fountain of our soul from bursting upon the visible world once its light radiates thousands of sparkles and once love propels us deep forward in our evolution.

Look at the sky and you will see fireworks, fires of joy that will sparkle for you... out of love and because of love, and simply for your eyes to marvel at. The marvel in your eyes is only the beginning of a process that will bring you pleasure, joy and hope. The cycle will continue with your mind and soul to bring you even more happiness.

We integrate our power of love by fully living in the present moment as it is and by respecting the universal synchronization in what we want to do. The mental impulses are brought back in place, in the frame they should be which is the guidance from the superior planes, and a balance that brings harmony installs itself. Others note this integration when we act justly and fairly and in harmony with the universal laws.

We are happy to serve which is different from serving to be happy.

The difference comes from unconditional to conditional love. It is feeling the joy of loving instead of loving to feel joy. We do not feel the need to try to gain the happiness we could feel by serving others, because we already feel a grand happiness even before serving. We are satisfied, fulfilled, and happy before we serve. Consequently, we expect nothing in return when we start serving others, because we miss nothing.

This suggests a certain independence and self-sufficiency in joy and pleasure, solely with ourselves. We can satisfy all our bodies and fulfill their needs without depending on others to achieve it.

As can be seen, serving others is not a goal, but a consequence of an accomplished work that consisted in building a solid foundation of harmony within ourselves. We don't have to be in action to create harmony, to find ourselves, and discover our basic characteristics as they are. It is fundamental to know and find ourselves before wanting to serve. If we don't, sooner or later, we will have difficulty to continue serving with detachment.

We do not orient ourselves towards service to realize who we are. Because we have already discovered how we really act, we choose the action of serving to materialize and assume ourselves further; to close the energy flow and live a certain fulfillment. Here are all the differences between the human roles and the universal or spiritual roles. The motivations that push us to act are very different. To appropriately serve humanity, we have no other choice than to play a spiritual and universal role. This role cannot be based solely on the human plane or be determined from individual and strictly human motivations.

Instead of serving in a personal manner, we serve others in a universal way, where our deep motivations transcend the individual plane to reach the collective one.

The peacefulness of the soul is necessary to serve others well.

To make amends by serving others is only an outlet that indicates that we have not yet made peace with ourselves, and that we haven't been able to forgive ourselves for some fault we might have committed.

It is from the outside that we run after peace. We do hope to be able to soon drown the guilt we feel by receiving the blessings of others who would forgive our faults. We do not have enough mercy to do it by ourselves on our own. We are saviors who look for victims to be rescued from persecutors.

We can not serve others on these foundations, because it is in fact ourselves we want to serve by using others to get there. Our intentions are not clear; detachment and the universal aspects of our deep motivations are clearly missing.

Being truly available to others is acquired by being available to ourselves. How can we be available to ourselves if we are not peaceful?... Until we are peaceful in our soul, we can not be available to ourselves or anyone else. We learn to be available by realizing what it brings when we aren't. We can then choose it with awareness. We can transcend any impulses that have pushed us to be savior, victim or persecutor.

It is mercy that brings peacefulness to the soul.

Only mercy allows the door to open, the door that leads to the universal role we want to play and the peacefulness of the soul we want to feel. To be merciful towards ourselves, we absolutely need to forgive ourselves without condition and without creating the need to make amends. This is critical. We even forgive our kids for their faults without them having to make amends or repairing their blunder. Why not do the same towards ourselves?

Let's stop feeling guilty and creating the need to make amends by appearing to be serving others. We can, right now, dissolve all of our feelings of guilt, thanks to the mercy we could feel for ourselves. Let us all do it since we all deserve it without exception!

Because of the love we will feel by doing that, we will return to happiness, recreate and re-invent it all by ourselves or on our own. We can all do that and it is under these conditions that we can adequately serve others and stop using them to serve ourselves, stop playing the human role of savior.

When we free ourselves from our hindrances to love, and our heart is full of tenderness and peace; when others only satisfy themselves with it... It is at this precise moment that making others happy makes us just as happy as if we were benefiting from the same favors from them. Our soul and theirs become one and the harmony is created in unison with the beyond.

This situation is very real and for us, it is not an abstract reality because more and more humans live this on earth. The individual surpassing leads us to genuine actions which are made out of love at the collective level. We then serve others in a universal way and with concerns that are directly related to the well-being of the entire collective. Our personal interests are put aside.

When love becomes very intense, it is easier to serve in a universal way.

Loving and being happy go together. Feeling the love of God and loving him naturally enrolls in the process of serving, once we have made peace with ourselves, and once we have reconciled our human and divine aspects. At the limit, serving others is serving God and when we feel love for God, serving becomes very easy and universal.

The soul is used as a conducting thread to reach God. Its divine intention is used by us as a spring board to achieve it and all becomes easy thereafter. Existing, acting or living on this earth takes a new sense and it is in joy that we have learned to live here... In the abandonment to all that is coming and for the well-being of all, including ourselves.

Dramas are stories of the past. Misfortune and burden no longer exist because our heart is wide open and love is a balm that heals any wounds that close themselves instantly. All is put in God's hands and accepted as he wants it.

We choose happiness with so much ease that being happy on earth becomes elementary and very simple. We only love without feeling the need to ask for anything else.

I am in love with the infinite love...

"I am in love... with the love that never ends... and never wants to end... I have a never ending love and I have also myself to love!...All together with what I have, we live the nicest romance!

With love and a heart to love, an open heart I should say, I need nothing more, because all I have is complete in itself. In fact, I have nothing else, and nothing is missing! Every thing else is a repetition of what I already have and it is really useless to name it once again. I have all I could hope for to be happy.

What must happen happens by itself without any help, and the superfluous always adds itself to what I am. The Universe places on my path what should be there in function of what I am, and it is all perfect this way. The battles of the past have become futile and are now over. Surrendering to the universe replaces these ways of doing things.

With my own re-birth and my "new self," I am capable of loving and I like doing it with my soul. I no longer need anything from the outside, because I draw my joy of living from my heart. In consequence, I like to serve and I like saying it to whoever wishes to hear it. I am at their service, to the service of God within themselves. I am ready to help them in respect of myself and them. All together, we form a team with God and the angels where none of us is excluded.

If you like, consider us as a headlight in a storm, and you will arrive safe and sound to the harbor!... My soul surrenders to the guidance from the beyond and my heart welcomes in this white light what we see on the horizon.

This light is available to all of us and nothing can stop it from shining."

Once we have truly detached ourselves, there is only ourselves with love left. Even if we are surrounded by others, only love remains. All the others only become pretexts to reveal and demonstrate our love in a very visible manner.

Achieving oneself in service brings fulfillment!

It is in surrender and abandonment that we achieve ourselves in serving others. This service consists in adding hope in the heart of all humans who seek light, while respecting, of course, what they choose to live. If the individuals who cross our paths prefer to continue to hate and suffer, we will not do anything that will go against their choice. We will look at them with compassion, wishing them "good luck" in everything they have chosen to experience. We want to contribute to the happiness of only those who desire and choose it. This is how we respect them and how I respect you. We are only here to love and for nothing else. That's my message to all that read this book.

Serving this way by surrendering ourselves to the Universe is a way of being that brings fulfillment, deep joy and grace. We overflow with joy and gratitude and we wish to share our feelings and our knowledge with others who surround us. We offer and surrender ourselves to help them become aware of themselves. We are not here to convince others or to promote beliefs, but to share with all who want to know how we continue learning to love and how we can live our life continuously in joy. We can help them feel more of the love that is sleeping deep within themselves. It is what we wish for them and it is by feeling intense love that we offer ourselves to you this way.

We are available to anybody and we invite all who seek the light and want love to come and meet with us. It is with humility, freely and without condition, that we offer our help to anyone who needs it. We need nothing in return, because we feel very good as we are and we already feel fulfilled with what we have. We experience a great happiness and it is more than sufficient for us. We have made peace with ourselves all the way to our souls.

This happiness becomes a part of us and forms a whole, like an entity together with us. All this, all that has been written corresponds to real, concrete and true situations that do happen on earth, here and now.

> *"I no longer have time to lose lying to myself, because I can not be happy by assuming such breaches to my authenticity. That is why I love to testify and demonstrate my inner truth as it is... In other words, declaring from my soul it's divine intention of love for all humanity. We only love and share our love and happiness with all who want to feel more of it. I wish that every human could feel the love and the peacefulness of his soul, and live a life of happiness."*

CHAPTER V EXERCISES

1. MEDITATION AIMING AT CREATING PEACE IN YOUR SOUL

- Take a few moments to visualize a vast ocean, a beautiful and calm sea. Look at all its splendor, the beauty of this expanse of water stretching out endlessly.

- Let the sound of the waves gently rock you. Hear the soft, steady and constant murmur that they create.

- In a cloudless and blue sky, imagine a bright sun shining its warm rays.

- Feel its invigorating heat that is penetrating you and realize how good it is to be there.

- Smell the fragrance coming from the magnificent beach on which you are resting, and really take the time to permeate yourself with the sense of well-being that it provides to please you.

- Breathe deeply in this feeling, so that it can totally fill all the cells of your body.

- Keep on breathing and contemplate how wonderful it is to be there, how wonderful it is to be alive in order to appreciate it.

- A few minutes later, take the time to fully realize what you have created with your emotions. You have just created this tremendous emotional well-being which brings peace to your soul. Take note of it now, remember and tell yourself that it could always be the case if you chose so.

- Really take the time to enjoy the quietness and the happiness that this meditation brought you, in order to remember it when your life will become more difficult to live. At this moment, you will then be able to take the time to go back to the same pleasant state of being that you have already experienced, and you will feel this sense of generalized well-being once more.

2. INTRODUCTION TO MAINTAIN PEACE AT ALL TIMES

- Let us continue with the previous exercise. Now, suppose that in this wonderful place where you are resting, a noisy motorcycle appears suddenly. How would you react? Focus on this event to introspect your inner-self. What will you choose to feel? See where you stand in your capability and aptitude at maintaining peace within yourself.

- Are you able to welcome this harsh noise, while remaining at peace within yourself? Can you see its positive side? Any one?... because there is always one.

- Are you able not to imprison yourself in this unexpected situation and not to be disturbed and pushed into bad feelings by this aggravating noise? To simply let it go?... Keep on seeing only what is good and beautiful, and to do this in order to simply continue to feel good about yourself.

- If you cannot maintain peace inside of you, what incites you to choose otherwise? Why do you do that? What incites you to resist peace?

- Have you not appreciated and fully embraced peace and happiness before this dreadful noise came about? Remember that you always have the choice to experiment and feel what you want.

- Why is your well-being only hanging by a thread?... Is hanging on to so little? Why do you surrender all your power to feel good to this motorcyclist?

- What do you have to learn in regard to this unwelcome visitor? Why has this situation occurred?

The same pattern is often reproduced in our daily lives when disturbing events happen or when situations happen to make us realize our errors or mistakes that we have made.

- Why not choose to maintain the peace at all times through mercy and compassion, instead of choosing non-forgiveness and to feel guilty? At the end, it only comes down to that. This motorcyclist is there only to make us realize where we stand in our capability to remain peaceful while living our daily life. Otherwise, it would not take so much importance...

"Stop giving away to others your power to feel good, and let you recover it from others. Cease blaming and indicting others to make them responsible for what has happened to you. This is how we distract ourselves from having forgotten what we have ourselves created and what we could have been!... It is not worth it!... Because, if our mind feels gratified, our heart, on the other hand, remains unsatisfied!

Be finally aware that there are always events that may be disturbing, and there always will be. It is up to us to choose if they will have or not a great or a small impact on how we feel and how we are. It is up to us to decide if they will be unsettling or not."

- Practice yourself, and in the long run, you will succeed as peace will be tamed and will become a faithful companion.

3. REFLECTIONS TO ESTABLISH PEACE THROUGH MERCY!

"A merciful and compassionate heart can transform into peace anything that can be disturbing and unsettling, in the life of any human being..."

- Remember having already forgiven someone in your life about an error or a fault he has made. Feel how good it made you feel inside. Realize it and allow yourself to really feel it, because this is how you become merciful and compassionate!

- Now, forgive "your motorcyclist" and wish for him a higher consciousness, and more light.

- Consider this situation as an opportunity of progress and learning to go further on the path of mercy, and to abolish your judgments and dissolve your guilt.

- Remember what you have felt while forgiving. As you have already been able to feel compassion and to forgive others, why would God, who is infinitely more merciful than you, not do the same for you for all the errors you could have made so far? Do not doubt about that! God has already accepted to forgive you. Otherwise, when you feel bothered by something, you would not be as conscious of it as you are now, and you would not become in a position to forgive yourself and to become merciful. Everything comes together in a love logic and it is up to you to choose it if you want to feel mercy, because you can immediately have access to it if you wish. Furthermore, if you are conscious of what precisely disturbs you, it is only to transform your way of being. Otherwise, you would not have been as aware of it as you are doing it so perfectly now. Why are you conscious of it? If it is not for healing it, healing the wounds which are related to it...

- Be aware of that and open your heart, in order to complete your healing. Welcome the mercy of God which will dissolve all the feelings of guilt in you. Because, behind every non-forgiveness or judgment that we carry within us, there is always this guilt that we project on others, and that we choose to maintain within ourselves. There is still this vision that the error or the fault is bad with all the dramas that we associate to it.

- Surrender your guilt or your non-forgiveness to God. Let them go. Transcend them in order to reach and feel the peace which is hiding behind them.

- At the outset, start with your mind and redefine the error in it, as a springboard to learn. Thereafter, go into your heart to soften yourself and to draw tenderness from it. This tenderness is a conducting thread that will lead you to this great reconciliation with all the components of your being; it will lead you to the compassion and the mercy that will eliminate any blocks that maintain what remains of non-forgiveness in yourself.

- Look after and cultivate mercy as you would for a beautiful garden that needs water and sunshine to flourish. The transcendence will thus be completed and peace will always triumph.

- Bathe yourself in mercy, because once you feel it, the mercy that God has for you and the mercy you have for others and for this noisy motorcyclist, to use our example, are, in fact, the same and only thing. Mercy is mercy as love is love. It is as simple as that!

The forgiveness to others, the forgiveness to yourself and the forgiveness from God are the same and only thing on the plane of your soul. It is to undertake this grand reconciliation in yourself and to integrate it in your entire physical body that you become aware of it and that you live it with your conscience.

- Accept this mercy in order to make it yours now, and see how good it is to revitalize yourself from it. While living your life, it will grant you with a grand happiness, grace and ecstasy.

- When this mercy fills and inhabits your heart, realize how easy it becomes to feel good about yourself! Realize how much you want to serve, and how much you feel gratified and happy in doing so. It is freely that you want to serve and without feeling obliged to do something for others.

4. PRACTICE TO BRING FORTH MERCY

- Do over the meditation of exercise number 1, but this time, include the sudden and shattering arrival of the motorcyclist.

- Reassure your ego by telling him that there is no more need to become agitated for so little and that this motorcyclist is not so important.

- Thank your ego for his patience, his understanding and his cooperation.

- With compassion, go draw from your soul the required mercy and compassion that will enable you to forgive.

- Let go of all guilty feelings, and tell your soul that there is no one guilty any longer and that all is perfect that way. All the events are perfect as they happen to you. There is no more non-forgiveness, as well as forgiveness, because you no longer function or reason on that basis and you no longer analyze life that way.

- Forget the motorcyclist. Whether he is present or not should not alter your sense of well-being. In fact, you have already reached the point where you are not hearing and seeing him anymore.

- Recover your power for feeling good and simply assume your well-being. Choose to continue to live it whatever happens.

Chapter VI

The Intention Of The Soul: Inciting Us To Love?...

We all have a soul that incites us to act in the sense of a grander personal and spiritual blossom. Our soul triggers the inner impulses that manifest themselves with feelings and vibrations in our physical body. Our intuition represent its voice, and we all have intuitions that reach our conscience at different times.

With these intuitions, our soul demonstrates its intention. It is then very important to pay attention to the messages it conveys in order to help us live our lives better.

What is the soul's intention?

The intention of the soul is that the human being becomes aware of his inner divinity for him to radiate unconditional love; of the love it sends outside, through all the components of this human for him to shine in the visible and physical world... The soul wishes for this individual to blossom and testify all the fulfillment he is capable of. And this, in the joy of living his life, in the joy of loving all that exists and in the sharing of his abundance, what he knows and has.

The intention of the soul is also its divine intentions; for the human being to assume the responsibility of his light and create his life with it; for him to rebuild and re-invent his life each day to always live more happiness. Since the soul has no ego, it only has good intentions that always comes down to an intention of unconditional love. It is wonderful, isn't it?...

To explain further, the intention of the soul is also motivating the human being to follow the plan of life that he has chosen before his incarnation. To help and lead him to achieve it and always go further; to support, sustain and make him capable of transcending from individuality to collectivity. And all this, for him to play, at the end, a universal role convenient and suitable for him, a role based on a well established solidarity with God, that it helps us to discover in all things.

> *"In my case, these impulses from the soul materialize and get all their senses by serving others... serving them with humility, joy and mercy. The service is like an outcome of what I have become and it allows me to live a greater fulfillment and more happiness... I have the liking to share with anybody what I know about love and happiness and you are most welcome."*

What do you do with the intentions of your soul?

What do you do with the intentions of your soul once they reach your conscience? Do you put them aside because your mind can't accept such suggestions coming from nowhere? Do they seem bizarre, lacking logic or making non-sense, at the extent of being afraid of being laughed at if you listen to them and adapt your behaviors in consequence?...

What happens with your potential of divinity?... Do you leave it there behind to vegetate?... Forgotten, abandoned and condemned to die by itself, like a prisoner from the internment camp?... Or, do you take action to assume it in your daily life?... The actions and the dispositions that could follow your intuition while not being afraid of the "what ifs?"

Once some of our dimensions or components want to live, but are condemned to die, interference and disharmonies follow in our behaviors and in our life. When we are least expecting it, our happiness is troubled and becomes blurred like leaves falling from a tree with autumn arriving in our life. We can stop seasons from changing and re-invent summer every day of our life, if we wish. Could you become aware of this situation to the extent of seeing clearly your disharmonies and the components of yourselves that suffer and want to live?...Seeing them with eyes of compassion in order to always support them in their evolution?

What goes on in your soul? What's inside of you, deep inside? Is there happiness or sadness? Do you have a tendency to be naturally happy or do you need to work hard to be? Is your soul extremely sad or is it filled with joy? The answer, of course, is in your soul, but it is in your life that you can see the consequences and the outcome and where you stand.

Do you act on the desires and wills of your soul?... What do you do, then, with its light? Does it transcend you to be visible for all or does it die on rocks like a wave of the sea? Do you prefer the influences of the immature or non-evolved astral entities to its light? Actually, this is really what's happening!... You can be sure of it! We choose between both: Between the radiant intuitions of our soul and the others which are less radiant... We can create our life with ego, which saddens our soul, or create our life with light, which makes it happy.

In what way is your soul useful?

Do you think its only role is to keep your physical body alive?... In fact, it is much more useful than that!... It is the soul who motivated your incarnation. And it has also conditioned the major events that go on in your life, and all this, to allow you to take spiritual lessons that you need to learn to be happier and widen your conscience.

Your soul is your best friend, your ally, a benefactor... A dimension of yourself that guarantees you happiness. No human being will ever love you as much as your soul does. And you, what do you do in return?... Do you send to your soul a little love back?

When was the last time you thanked your soul? Are you aware that it's your soul who is responsible for you being alive? That it's only your soul that supports you at all times, even if you don't realize it!

Your soul is worthy of love... of your love. The more you will love it and feel its love, the more you will be able to love, because you will only feel love, without understanding, without thinking, without having a logical reason and without having anything on the outside to justify such ways of being. It is amazing, isn't it?

**Even if you ignore it,
your soul only loves and supports you.**

You have access to your soul, like an immense source of love and joy. Go and draw from it when you are eager to satisfy yourself with love and joy. Do it each time you feel the desire or the inclination for it.

Love is available within you; you only need to want this love and go get it. It is there just waiting for you to make you happy. It is no where else but deep within yourself, ready to make your happiness as you wish it to be and with full respect of yourselves. If you only want a little love, you will only feel a little. If you want more, you can have more. It is as you wish and that's why we can always respect our soul because it always respects us.

We all have a soul that feeds our very human heart with divine and unconditional love, and because our divine and human dimensions are reconcilable in all times, we are all capable of loving with our soul... All without exception.

You are all capable of reflecting in a visible way and with excellence this intense love that rests deep within you. Stop underestimating yourselves to see at what extent you are able to love. This underrating is only a learning process that will lead you to better appreciate yourself and to feel more love at the end. Your sleeping love is like a gigantic fountain that waits only for your signal to burst out and flourish your inner scenery more, the marvelous garden of your heart.

All around, other wonderful gardens are missing revival. Let us be their sun and their beneficial rain like in the gardens of our own heart. Let your fountain burst out so life can resume everywhere and make miracles!

Our souls have the talent to bring to life again all that is dying within ourselves. Our souls are like good fairies that wait for us to transform all sadness and sorrow in an immense happiness. To make it happen, we only have to ask sincerely for it.

Is the soul capable of human warmth?

The evolved soul of some people is sometimes more human than other persons can be or are towards themselves, and that is what is paradoxical. How can the soul include this comprehension, this compassion and this warmth that is very human?...It can only be the case when it loves the fundamental of the human being and all humans without conditions... And this, because it has no ego. To have as much compassion, it must accept the presence of God within it and wish only happiness for everyone.

My soul wishes for all of you to live in joy and light, and it is with joy that I transmit to you its message of love and best wishes of happiness. Nothing in me can stop these messages from being transmitted.

Becoming divine to love our human dimensions!...

I thank my soul which has taught me to love without judging my human reactions. Because demonstrating and making alive our human side also holds all its beauty, the beauty of learning to go further within ourselves, and all the marvels there are about existing to be able to do so. Being "human" is just as perfect in itself as being "divine," because it is a part of ourselves that also has its reasons for being! It manifests itself in a visible way, at the right time and when it is necessary; when certain of our aspects need to be recognized and taken care of to evolve.

The soul is like the captain of a boat. Without this helm, I would drift away. Thanks to my soul, I can continue steering for loving at all times and appreciating myself as I am. We don't need to admit the presence of our soul for this to happen. However, if we deny its presence, it will be more difficult to achieve.

Once we reduce our identity, only to our human dimensions, and forget that we also have a soul, it becomes sometimes harder to love ourselves as we are with all our human reactions. By enlarging our ways of being to include the divine dimensions of our soul, our vision of things becomes wider, so much that we can easily love our human reactions, no matter how immature they are. We then realize that we are only learning something that we don't already know, but we will know and master soon.

We assemble all that happens to us and all our human reactions in a much larger context and it makes it easier to give sense to our reactions and all that happens. Once we do not recognize the presence of our soul, we cannot give a sense to many things that happen to us. We can't find any logical interpretation and it is much more difficult to live our life that way, to live it in joy.

On another more fundamental or even more simple plane that is attached to all that we live and how we react, we notice that we only learn to love at all times. It all comes down to always learning to love a little more each day. Especially, when we make mistakes, we learn because we enlighten our beliefs and lose some of our illusions. Others are here to help us in that purpose. We are also here to do our "work" which consists of learning to love by experiencing some of our human reactions. Towards others, the roles are reversed, and the coordination of all that happens is done by God and the angels according to the needs of our souls to evolve.

**All that we live
is related to our apprenticeship in love.**

Our human reactions are always connected to a new apprenticeship about love. All this happens on purpose that we come to a position to love better all that exists at all times. It is our ultimate goal.

This is what happens at a more elevated and subtle level of ourselves, on a less obvious plane, but very real. There is always a perfect matching between the events of the visible Universe which happens in our lives and the learning that progresses on the loving plane, on our aptitude to love that transforms itself. All is played in function of what we need to understand or feel to be in a position to love better.

To notice this reality, we only need to look further within ourselves, to look with the eyes of our conscience. At this particular moment, we realize that it makes all its sense.

> *"All that I have lived has been useful to learn to love. None of my sufferings were in vain and none of my small happy times either.*
>
> *... And if today, I am capable of loving all that exists with more fervor, it is thanks to all I have lived yesterday, the day before and so on... No human being can escape this universal rule of spiritual growth, even the ones who aren't aware of it."*

CHAPTER VI EXERCISES

1. FOUNDATION FOR RECOGNIZING THE INTUITION COMING FROM YOUR SOUL

The inner silence is the appropriate ground for the manifestations of our intuitions. With practice, everyone can achieve some results. Relaxation is another tool which helps our intuitions to reach our conscience, because it allows the mind to slow down its activities. It is important for the mind to slow down in order to allow the voice of our soul to be heard within ourselves. It is one or the other.

Meditation is another privileged tool that leads to a deeper understanding and realization of the meaning of an intuition.

- To begin a meditation, choose a quiet place where you will not be disturbed.

- Gather and bring yourself to a state of calmness and deep relaxation.

- Focus your attention on your inner light, and visualize it for a few seconds.

- Create the conditions for the silence taking place within yourself, feel it, and go back to the source of your thoughts.

- To come to the point where you lessen your thoughts or you think on a less frequent basis, use your conscience to focus on the images that appear inside of you. At the same time, it will help you to slow down your mind and this is what you are looking for.

- If a thought arises, just let it move on without effort and visualize a white screen. We know that you may find it difficult to discipline your mind at the beginning, but with regular practice it will become easier and you will continuously improve yourself.

- Observe and identify what happens between two thoughts. Be alert to what occurs because a message may be conveyed to you; an image may suddenly appear on your inner screen.

- Notice the differences between the thoughts that are brought and produced by your mind and the messages or the images sent by your soul to your conscience. There is a tremendous chance that all that is not of a mental essence is the outcome of your soul.

- Identify what occurs when you use your will, and what happens independently of your will. For example, you know something all of a sudden without any explanation as to how or why you have this knowledge. Images appear in your head without you controlling them. You hear something like a voice talking to you, revealing something or leading you toward a specific area of your life that needs guidance and improvement toward love. This occurs regardless of any effort coming from your will or your mind, and it is your soul that is making a direct contact with you.

- After 15-20 minutes, put an end to your meditation.

- If you obtain very little result, just take it easy and start over another day when you will be more rested and in a better mood for it. Continue and be sure that, one day, good results will materialize.

- If you have already obtained some results, use your mind as well as your conscience to deepen your understanding on what you have experienced during your meditation.

- Analyze and identify your results in order to bring out:

1) The thoughts corresponding to what has been decided by you, with your will, or that have been created by your mind; those that are stemming from circumstances or from some outside events in your life. For example, when you choose to think of something in particular, these thoughts do not derive from your soul.

2) The thoughts, intuitions, messages or images that appear without any reason or without being aroused by anything that could create them; those that are not induced or chosen by your mind and by you because of an outside stimulus. The latter are generally created when your mind is less active or while you are in a deep state of relaxation and peace.

- Make out the differences between the two. It is very important, because in this manner, you will become clearer with what goes on inside yourself. As time goes by, you will come to a position to establish a reliable network of communication between your soul and your conscience.

Practice! Practice yourself often! It is all a question of time before you succeed. And even though you would not succeed on the first attempt, what does it really matter? It has not much importance, since you are in the process of learning it, and this is what counts.

2. EXERCISE TO VERIFY IF YOU FOLLOW THE LIFE PLAN OF YOUR SOUL

1st STEP: THE EGO

- Act as if your entire being is only your ego.

- Identify the human aspects that characterize the person you are.

- Inspire yourself with your human aspects in order to make out your ego's life plan. What does your ego want?

- How does the life plan of your ego fit into the life plan of your entire being? What place do you allow it to have?

2nd STEP: THE SOUL

- Act as if your entire being is only your soul.

- Identify the divine aspects that characterize the person you are.

- Inspire yourself with your divine aspects in order to make out your soul's life plan. What does your soul want?

- How does the life plan of your soul fit into the life plan of your entire being? What place do you allow it to have?

3rd STEP: TO SUMMARIZE

- What really happens in practice? Which life plan do you follow in your daily life?

- In your life, do the two plans merge together? Differ from one another? Are similar? Complement one another?

- What is the true identity of your entire being? Closer to your ego or to your soul?

The ideal would be for the two life plans to be identical, and that, in your every day life, you follow the plan that fulfills and matches the most with the criteria and the needs of your soul.

Your human identity could then be the result of the harmony, the merging of your human aspects together with your divine ones. This fusion is done at the level of your heart which would then be made up only of love and of light.

As a consequence, be sure that a great and lasting happiness will take place. A happiness so great that you even cannot imagine it now!

CONCLUSION

A book on love can only be concluded with happiness. Happiness is what we all look for. Happiness is built on the simplest things of life. Love is always present in it. How can it be any other way? Difficult to imagine!

Without love, the recipe is missing one ingredient. Without love, life is more dull. Without love, what do we have left? Not much, not much at all in fact... Very little to console us... Only illusions and temporary joys that always go and fade away... They fade away as fast as they came.

With love, happiness is a certainty. It is assured because it becomes permanent. With love, we acquire the certainty that we will always feel good about ourselves and will still feel it tomorrow. As long as human beings look for light, there will be hope because this is how they will continue learning to love themselves. And by loving, all becomes possible. With love, we can obtain all we could hope for and be fulfilled at all levels.

In fact, on this earth, only love exists at different degrees. Love is present in everything and in different ways. It is malleable and takes the appropriate form.

Any human or anything can be a pale reflection of love or one of its grandiose manifestations. We only need to look with the eyes of the heart to visualize the love that all that exists contains, to see the love it conceals, if it is not directly visible. We see love in different ways depending on the progress we have made in our apprenticeship to love. We can be unable to see it, or become in a position to see it a lot and everywhere, once our liking or inclination to love is amplified.

There is always equivalency and matching between the power or the source of love that our heart accepts from our soul and the love we can discover on the outside. The interrelationship is always maintained. We limit ourselves on the inside, not by the outside which is its consequence. Everyone chooses on his own how much love he accepts to see on the outside. We choose as well the limits of our happiness and of our suffering as they are related to our ability to see and feel love. We are capable to stop any suffering at all times, but it is up to us to truly want it.

All that exists is here to love and be loved... To contribute to our happiness and to the ones of others. Now there is the true sense of life. By definition, all that exists is a source of happiness. We dry up this source once we stop drawing love from within ourselves...

Each human is here to add a little more color to love depending on his style and his differences. Each human enrolls in this process with a definite place that is reserved for him and with his full potential of creativity, to create and re-create love and happiness in his own way... Because we are all masters of art and we have the full control on our happiness and our life. We have the perfect control on our ego and we are all capable to dominate all suffering.

It's like a party where we are all invited, the ball of love. We can be a poor dancer or a sensational one and it is always up to us to choose what we want to be, to choose our role. We can choose to take our place or to even refuse this invitation.

I thank God and the angels for all the graces and the immense joy they have gratified me with. Thank you for all this abundance! Thank you for allowing me to live all that has happened to me! Thank you for the angers and the sorrows!

Also, I thank all of you faithful companions! It is with courage that you have come down here, like me, in the physical world to learn to love further. There is a lot to marvel at in front of the greatness of all you have already accomplished! Thank you! Thank you very much!

Gilles Deschênes
Montreal, Canada
Tel: (514)-982-9582

APPENDIX

The Illustration Of A Universal Law

Attack always brings its counter-attack.

To fully understand this statement, we have to begin with identifying and discerning the motives that push a person (the attacker) to attack another (the attackee), and explain what is meant by attack.

First, the attack can happen in the invisible Universe, by our thoughts and attitudes that we address to others at their mental and emotional levels. This kind of assault is frequent and can even become very aggressive and irritating in the long run. When a person continuously directs aggressive thoughts towards another, the latter can feel harassed when she thinks about the former. This discomfort constitutes concrete demonstrations of her successful attacks. This kind of attack can be neutralized if the attackee chooses it and responds with love thoughts.

The attack can also manifest itself by physical blows that can be seen in the visible Universe. The "blows" can be from words that we use to discredit the "attackee" towards a third party. In business, it can take the form of actions aiming to ruin our competitors. Finally, the most elementary manifestations of an attack are physical blows that can be given to the physical body of our enemy.

We also need to enlarge our field of comprehension and fully realize what we are doing when we attack others.

Because, we are often not aware of what we do and we act on impulse. The energy behind this type of very human reaction has not yet been harmonized and integrated in the deep areas of our being. We need to learn some lessons and our reactions show it clearly.

Once the attacker and the attackee reply to each other, the combat degenerates and a war is created.

What is attacking others?

Attacking others is creating conditions of counter-attacking and preparing the ground and the space of counter blows we will inevitably be subjected to!.. Because if there is attack, there are also quarrelsome urges and impulses and the dynamic of the process has been well triggered. The necessary energy for war has been brought and the progress logically follows its course. The counter attack is only another inevitable stage, another one of its manifestations because the conscience has not yet created the conditions that could make it gush out the necessary energies for peace.

War can happen on a small scale (between two people) or on a larger level (between groups of people).

The counter-attack could come from elsewhere than from the one who has undergone your attack, if this enemy you have aimed for no longer wants to fight. Be assured that your aggressing attitude and your ways of doing things will find a buyer or taker somewhere in the universe and reactions will follow... Aggressiveness always attracts its reciprocal and the cycle of attack/counter-attack will continue on its own, as long as we will maintain the illusion we support concerning the sense we make of the events that incite us to quarrel, as long as we will not have surpassed and transcended the state of the soul that is linked to it.

Even if we make war, our soul, deep within, is only looking for peace.

At the soul's level, there are no wars; there is no distinction between friends or enemies. This way of seeing things is based on mental concepts created at the human level and maintained by some of our dimensions that still need to learn and blossom... We still need to enlarge our understanding of what happens to us... See farther with more awareness.

By looking at all that happens in the frame of this more vast perspective, we notice that we only have, in fact, allies and collaborators that have accepted before their incarnation, to play different roles in our life.

Some have chosen to play unappreciated roles, because they love us enough to choose pushing aside their personal and human interests to place priority on the evolution of our soul. Consequently, many agitations and confrontations arise at the personality level designed to bring necessary adjustments to our soul's greatest deficits.

Others play a role that is more in agreement with our personalities and there is less conflict on the physical plane. It is all possible, all by serving their soul and ours. It all depends on what our soul needs to evolve, because this is how the scenario is created and the actors choose to participate in it. This all happens that way in order to make evolved our fundamental components and to make sure that it will no longer be the caprices of our personality that will be considered as deep motivations of all our life and all our being.

At a more universal level, there is only apprenticeship, conditions and lessons of life that are created, recreated or that are undone and unknotted on their own, once all has been learned and integrated, once all the roles have been played completely.

Then why go to war?...

Going to war against someone who is finally here to help us see clearer within ourselves... A war that has nothing to do with what incites us to fight on the outside... A war that feeds itself on all the inner conflicts that still subsist within ourselves, conflicts that we refuse to see but which need to be resolved. Notice the perfect matching; our inner conflicts melt and merge themselves together with the war that we look for on the outside, because there is a natural attraction. By sincerely facing up to these conflicts, we could learn to dissolve them on our own, without needing a war on the outside. Because, if it would be this way, we would demonstrate peace in our relationships with others, instead of war that could then lose all its sense. The natural attraction and the perfect matching between what happens inside and outside are always met. This is a universal law.

How can we stop new attacks?...

> *"If you really want to prevent a new attack from being directed towards you and if you want to neutralize your so-called 'enemy,' then DON'T ATTACK HIM WHEN YOU ARE IN A POSITION TO DO SO!"*

How can we do this? By simply creating within ourselves the necessary conditions to make the energy of peace gush out... A peace that could shine and radiate all around us and reach others at the level of their heart. We then feel that we have no more enemies, only people who are put in our paths to make us learn to love in all sorts of circumstances.

"Instead of spreading war on the outside once again, make peace with yourself. Look in your heart to see what you can find; It is your lack of love that maintains your inner combats... And the war you are pursuing is your own war. It is the one you transpose on the outside; it has started no where else but within you!

Your bogus friends are only nice pretexts that allow what is hiding in your heart to show itself in the physical world. This is how we can see your true colors and you can notice them to come to finally recognize your deepest feelings, what you truly are.

If your enemies came to you as friends, they will stimulate within you the energy of peace rather than the one that feeds your inner and own war. In these conditions, would you be able to recognize and acknowledge by yourself your own unbalances? Admit with me that it would be much harder... Your disharmonies and unbalances are very well hidden and as long as they are kept secret, you will not be able to live with peacefulness, balance and harmony on a lasting basis. Your enemies are there only to help you to become aware of it. As soon as you will end your own war, you will realize all their usefulness. They have only crossed your path to help you learn how to be at peace in all sorts of external conditions.

Install peace and compassion in your heart because that is where the real conflict needs to be settled... And this is how the need to attack others will die. This is how you will stop doing it and others will be able to start coming towards you with peace...like being tamed, attracted and pushed by a new impulse that you would have created.

Once you have settled this internal conflict, it is with ease that you will avoid undertaking warlike actions and this, even if the one who has made you angry, unbalanced or frustrated had attacked you first, and even if you are now in a position to demolish him once and for all with a good chance he would never recover.

From a mental point of view, it is tempting to believe under these circumstances that a definite victory in the physical world would settle the problem once and for all. Know that it is not the case and it is certainly not by attacking your enemy that you will be able to neutralize the quarrelsome and aggressing impulses that you generate yourself. On the contrary! Since you maintain, project and demonstrate them on the outside, you will be able to revive them in him! And if he doesn't do anything with them, you will wake up hostile attitudes in someone else, somewhere else in the invisible Universe and new attacks will certainly follow.

Action brings reaction.

Someone else will choose you as a target, because it is you who chooses war as a way of acting and you are the source that continues to feed the conflicts on the universal plane... And in our visible world, it is only a question of time before you learn at your own expense what will be his reaction, the hostile demonstrations that will materialize towards you. All this so you can further realize what results in creating war... the conflict you create and maintain first in yourself. All this happens naturally, like an automatic mechanism: 'action-reaction,' because this is the law. You can finally see who you are from the outside, since you have demonstrated and expressed this need and you don't do it on your own from within.

Let go of the one you can't see any other way but as an enemy. Get him out of your claws! Stop the fighting and let him live, exist and learn in his own way... make his own mistakes and be mistaken... Because this is the type of attitude you create for yourself from others, and this is how you will invent tolerance, peace and love for yourself, originating from elsewhere and other sources than yourself..."

There is always a buyer or a taker somewhere in the invisible world for what we are and as we are. There are no exceptions.

We choose peace by abandoning our own war towards ourselves.

"Choose now that others be takers and buyers of peace towards yourself instead of war! What do you desire for your future? Another war... more wars or peace and always more peace?...

Choose now!...

Peace is easy to live with, and it will immediately make you reach happiness. On the other hand, war is more difficult and more painful to support, because of the anguish and suffering it brings and the confusion it creates. You can be sure that a work of neutralization and pacification will be done in the invisible Universe, if you choose peace facing this privileged target you qualify as an enemy and who is now in a position of weakness towards you... that you consider, in fact, as a prey so vulnerable and so easy to conquer and eliminate.

If you act as predator, be ready in return to be pursued as a prey. But if you choose peace instead, there will be nothing in the invisible Universe to incite your enemy to attack you again or counter-attack, even if he could one day be in a position to do so and get revenge.

As a consequence of your choice, you can be sure he will do nothing against you in the visible Universe. It is the same towards any other potential enemy that could be tempted to engage hostilities with you. You disarm them in the invisible Universe and the consequence follows in our visible world. It is the LAW OF CAUSE AND EFFECT, WHICH IS AN INFALLIBLE AND UNCHANGEABLE UNIVERSAL LAW, *that will prevail for sure as soon as you will fully learn the lesson of compassion aimed towards peace, as soon as you will choose peace with the awareness of what you do."*

Experiencing war is a means that allows us to learn how to make peace.

It is one way to learn, the hard way...

"Starting other battles and continuing the war in order to finally make peace reign is only a big illusion... An illusion you can surpass by answering war with peace, instead of with war again. And if you come to react this way, it is because you have enough love in your heart; your heart is open enough to incite you to put an end to all hostilities. Even if the war can be won and end in a decisive victory in our visible Universe, it will never bring true and lasting peace, as long as you will have not really chosen and preferred peace to war. The hostilities will not be finished on all planes and the war will continue in other dimensions. It is only a question of time before it

overflows under other forms in our physical world, because it is only peace that can put an end to it in the invisible Universe. It is critical to truly choose peace to put an end to the war in all the Universes.

Choosing peace, is creating within ourselves an oasis of peace from which we can feed at all times.

All your bogus enemies will set you free in their thoughts. They will stop hostilities if you persevere this way and reinvent peace every time it is needed. They will quit the fight and abandon their aggressive impulses towards you, by realizing what you have become and what is the new situation... the peacefulness you reflect... the peacefulness you have installed in your heart... the oasis of peace you offer them.

Attacking is creating conditions for counter-attack to take place. Get out of this vicious circle by choosing to put an end to hostilities. Put your sword in its sheath and your assailant will do the same. It is only a question of time before he does so. He will not have a question of time before he does so. He will not have the occasion nor the desire to use it against you."

This is how peace triumphs and replaces war in the heart of all who were angry with us not so long ago. All this begins in our heart which must first of all, be open to peace. Every human being is capable to act out of peace, even though all his neighborhood incites him to make war.

"If you act this way, you will become this great leader who will have triggered a new process of peace, and who knows where this peace will bring you! Because, once peace is installed this way, it will reign and influence others all around you.

Consider yourself a hero, because it takes a lot of courage and love to choose and install peace, when the outside incites you to war and you find a golden opportunity to give a good lesson to your worst enemy, to give him the blow of grace! This is where we recognize your true power, the power of the peace you choose... the goodness and the generosity you allow yourself, in fact... From now on, you will be able to reflect this goodness in everything you do, because the peace that takes root in your heart stimulates your inclination to be better and to testify it in the visible world. Your goodness is like a logical extension of this grand peace and good faith that you have chosen in front of your enemy. It is now ready to produce its fruits."

Peace only brings victory and makes everybody a winner!

"If you desire it, you and your enemy could even come to the point of celebrating the triumph of peace over war, because you are both winners and there are no more losers when choosing peace! By making peace and cultivating it, you will both win in return. You will both win more prosperity rather than destruction."

Facing the competitors I could eliminate in the management of my business, I choose to look at them with compassion and peace. I abandon all combat while wishing them to contact light. I even praise their qualities when I have the opportunity to do so. The outcome is that my business benefits from unmatched prosperity. As the years go by, a link of friendship and respect has been created with all my competitors that I now consider like "my brothers in the abundance," this abundance that is only asking to be shared and that, in fact, comes from God.

Since I have been able to concretely realize the results of making peace, I have extended the universal principles to other sectors of my life. Each time, it has proved to be fair and brought me great satisfactions, a stronger peacefulness assorted always with happiness.

I, who have made war so many times and at the price of so much suffering, I choose peace and I renew my choice each day that goes by, while living a great happiness.

The war is over!

Now, it is unarmed that we present ourselves to you with love in our hearts and with peaceful intentions... and this peace, we visualize it for the whole planet. With good will, we can make peace reign... Make it shine everywhere around us by our actions as good examples.

We believe in the benefits of peace and we have put aside the destructive effects of war as a way of facing obstacles we meet while living our life. We wrap all these obstacles with peace and love, and send them to the Universe to put them in the hands of God. Thanks to this attitude, we can live our daily life without worrying and we incite to peace people who come towards us.

Revolutions and war bring about only little changes.

The wars and revolutions that happen in our world don't often change the hearts; they don't fill them with peace and love. They don't bring the true changes and the well-being that the people hoped for. Of course, there are physical changes, economic or political system changes. We do not deny this, but all these only give an illusion of changes and perpetuate it. Afterwards, we often realize that these wars or revolutions are all alike, and that there really wasn't true change at the end, the change we were expecting at the very beginning... Only transformations on the physical plane, without transforming the hearts or the behaviors and mentalities that reflect them.

In consequence, the hearts that remain unsatisfied are always seeking for the well-being and the peace that wasn't found in the changes in the physical world. The peacefulness of the heart can not be invented from the outside, but from within ourselves and it is ONLY IN THE HEART THAT TRUE CHANGES CAN HAPPEN. That is where peace is played, where love that makes its roots replaces hate which feeds the needed energy for war.

Peace starts in the heart and the only true and lasting change that brings peace is the one of the heart. This happens when love takes root and triumphs over hate and when peace replaces all our inner conflicts that have created "our own war", a war we have simply exteriorized and projected on others, usually without realizing it.

The changes in the heart are the true revolutions!

These changes, once they are directed towards more harmony and more peace, always bring grand satisfactions. The transformations on the physical plane that follow reflect the love and the peace of the ones who have already transformed themselves at their heart's level. These transformations are more gratifying at the collective level than the ones that political revolutions or wars can bring because they are usually unable to change the hearts.

GLOSSARY

The chakras are the centers that every human being has and uses to capture the energy he needs to live his life. These centers feed, regulate or harmonize with their energy, our different bodies: physical, emotional, mental, spiritual, extra-sensory etc... There are seven major chakras that are spread from top to bottom of our spinal cord and form our channel: the chakra of the crown, the third eye chakra, the chakra of the throat, and the chakra of the heart are the superior chakras. The solar plexus chakra, the hara chakra, and the base chakra are the inferior chakras.

The bodies are different planes or dimensions of ourselves in the visible or invisible Universe; the notion of bodies I am referring to includes the mental body, the emotional body, the physical body and the other energetic bodies such as the astral body for example.

The ego is an energy that allows us to develop our human potential and to assume our human dimensions. We learn with it to come to the awareness of our interior divinity and to also assume it. Ego is related to unawareness and this energy becomes love when it reaches maturity.

The personality is mainly formed of the mental and emotional bodies without restricting to them. These bodies represent some of our dimensions in the invisible Universe. The personality represents what a human has become at one point of his evolution. The personality constantly evolves and the ego animates it, until that moment when he reaches what he aims to become, i.e. love, as it is in our soul. The human dimensions are the ones of the physical body and the personality.

Our components or our dimensions are all our bodies, all our chakras and our soul. They can also be represented by sub-categories of the above.

A spirit or spiritual guide is the equivalent of your guardian angel. He protects you and watches over your physical and spiritual well-being. He helps you live your life better. He is the guardian of the plan of life that your soul has chosen to follow before its incarnation. He is always in touch with your soul and you can directly contact him, because his vibrations are perfectly compatible with yours.

A master of light is a purified and very luminous soul (incarnated or not). It is the equivalent of an angel who would have acquired a great power of love. Its goal is to spread love on earth, to make the collective conscience evolve and assist humans who want to undertake a universal mission.

The guidance of beyond is a set of messages and intuitions that are sent to our soul from our guardian angels, from spiritual guides or disembodied masters of light. The information transmitted to us is structured in systems in function of a very precise theme that we wish to learn. For example: goodness. We can logically deduct that we are guided, by being alert to the types of thoughts that spontaneously reach our conscience.

The Universe represents all the visible and invisible forces and all that exists.

God is the supreme energy that governs all that exists in the visible and invisible Universe; the strength or power that dominates all that can exists; it is the source of all life; the big boss of all. It is concentrated energy of love, light in a pure state, infinite goodness, mercy without limits and all the happiness we could imagine.

The soul is constituted with light which could be of various intensities. It is a parcel of this divinity mentioned above, an immortal breath of life, with an unlimited potential for love. It is the source of life that animates each human being, deep within himself.

The universal laws are a way to explain all that happens on the human plane, but by adding a spiritual dimension to it and by taking into account the invisible reality and the beyond, their causes and their effects in the material world. They provide a more complete explanation of all that happens. For example, if we always keep our heart open, we will be able to love at all times and this love will definitely attract the love of others. Love that attracts love is an unchangeable universal law and is well known on every continent.

The material, the material world or the material things represent all that is tangible, all that we can see or touch in the Universe.

The "non-loving" represents everything that is not love and that is not loving.

The "non-forgiveness" is everything that is not forgiveness, everything that contributes to the refusal to forgive. This can include feelings, emotions, attitudes, reasonings, etc...

The mercy is an energy that contains vibrations of love, kindness, tenderness and compassion, and which enables us to forgive unconditionally, regardless of the error or fault committed. Among other things, this energy enables us to dissolve the feeling of guilt that a human being uses to judge, indict and project his guilt on others and to maintain the non-forgiveness in himself. It eliminates the need to repair or to make amends for faults or errors that have been committed. It makes forgiveness an automatic reflex and it is like a balm that mends the wounds of the soul which goes back to peace and to joy. We eliminate the need to seek for guilt in others as mercy changes our vision.

The compassion is an energy similar to mercy, that allows us to soften and sympathize with ourselves or with others. We can put ourselves in the place of another to better understand him, and to feel sympathy for him. We can adopt the same attitude if it concerns us. We will then be in a position to understand ourselves better without needing others to cooperate with us in order to do that. Compassion does not necessarily imply the need to forgive and dissolve the guilt, because it acts on other levels of emotions to re-establish the peace. For example, it is very useful to surpass our fears and anguish, and heal the suffering caused by some life situations that we have difficulty to live with serenely in our daily life.